GAIN FROM PAIN

GAIN FROM PAIN

God's purposes are always good

JANET GOODALL

GILEAD
B O O K S
PUBLISHING

Gilead Books Publishing
Corner Farm
West Knapton
Malton
North Yorkshire
YO17 8JB UK
www.GileadBooksPublishing.com

First published in Great Britain in 2020
2 4 6 8 10 9 7 5 3 1

Copyright © Janet Goodall 2020

British Library Cataloguing-in-Publication Data:
A catalogue record for this book is available from the British Library.

ISBN-13: 978-1-9997224-5-6

All rights reserved.
No part of this publication may be reproduced, stored in a retrieval system or transmitted in any form or by any means, electronic, mechanical, photocopying, recording or otherwise, without the prior permission of the publisher.

Unless stated otherwise, scriptures are taken from The Holy Bible, New International Version®, NIV® Copyright © 1973, 1978, 1984, 2011 by Biblica, Inc.
® Used by permission. All rights reserved worldwide.

Typesetting and cover design by Dona McCullagh.

Cover image © Katelynn DiCarlo www.pursuingpearls.com

*For Jennie Chapman and Dick-with-Sarah Bowen.
I am deeply grateful for all that they have taught me.*

Contents

PREFACE IX
ACKNOWLEDGEMENTS XIII
INTRODUCTION XV
ABBREVIATIONS XVIII

1.	Pain comes to us all	1
2.	Love's labour rewarded	11
3.	Not worth living—or of great value?	17
4.	Burdens can break or make	29
5.	Entering the valley: scared or serene?	39
6.	The paradox of pain: If God is almighty, why does he allow it?	49
7.	The paradox of pain: If God is love, how can he bear it?	61
8.	There is always a good reason for God's delays	71
9.	Pain when gain is the chief aim	79
10.	Waste or worship?	89
11.	Faith on trial	101
12.	From not loved to beloved	111
13.	From darkness to light	119
14.	Hope at wits' end corner	129
15.	Never the same again	139
16.	The productivity of pressure	149
17.	Storing up treasure in heaven	159
Last word		169

Preface

MANY YEARS ago, I worked for a time in the United States of America. When meeting people new to me I was impressed by the way they introduced themselves by name and sometimes added their professional background. Well, my name is on the cover but I'd better explain my background.

I undertook medical training at Sheffield University and later specialised as a children's doctor. I have practised as a paediatrician in the UK, America and Uganda. In 1990, I retired from hospital practice in England and travelled more widely. A particular emphasis in my teaching has been how young children view what is happening around them, from birth to death. In many places I found this to be an important gap in medical education, as it had largely been in mine. Looking back on my own early childhood I still recall some of my unspoken misconceptions—helpful now when trying to see through a child's eyes, and even applicable to some adults.

The summer that I left school as a teenager, my mother died of cancer. As a young Christian I had fervently prayed for her healing, although she had been clear-eyed about what was happening and put her trust in the God of love, believing that she was on the way from her home to his. My father shared her faith and was able to support her in it despite his own great sadness. As she deteriorated and was in some discomfort our kind family doctor came and, as he knew me to be a prospective medical student, enlisted my aid. In those days, to relieve pain in the home, a tablet of morphine was dissolved in a teaspoonful of water, warmed by a burning match underneath it and the resultant solution injected. My job was to hold the spoon and match steady as the doctor did the rest, gradually bringing relief to his patient. She died peacefully at home with her family at the bedside. A few weeks later I entered medical school.

It seems likely that the memory of this experience, together with the pain of the ensuing bereavement and uprooting, lay dormant for years. In time it no doubt played a part in my growing concern for disabled and dying children and their brothers and sisters. I have witnessed bereavements of different kinds in many other lives besides my own. The chief lesson learned has been that, when given to God and supported by others, there can be gain from our pain. Given time, that gain may turn into treasure to be shared.

I am grateful to those who have shared their varied experiences with the rest of us. I am also conscious of the many who still struggle with their sufferings and have, as yet, no sense of gain but know only loss. It is my hope that the stories of some who have come through their trials will encourage troubled people to keep on keeping on. One day may they, too, be enabled to look back and trace how the love of God has sustained them throughout their struggles. He always has a creative purpose in mind and will never leave or forsake us.

I have written of lessons learned on the way, aware that reminders have often been needed to look for them. There will doubtless be more to come as God's intention for each of us is a work in progress until we finally go to join him. Then we shall at last perfectly reflect his likeness.

A NOTE ON BIBLE REFERENCES

Bible references are included in the text where appropriate. Selected references are included at the end of each chapter for readers wishing to meditate further.

Acknowledgements

SOME WHO have contributed to my thoughts in this book are unknown to me personally and some are no longer alive to be thanked. They have blessed us by showing patient endurance under pressure.

I am grateful to Dr Mark Haughton, Jeremy Lefroy, Dr Janet Lefroy, Dr Valerie MacKay, Revd Shaun Morris, Mrs Margaret Sentamu and Professor John Wyatt who have each read and commented on parts of the script, which has been so much appreciated. Revd Martin Oram unwittingly provided the subtitle in a twice repeated phrase in a sermon. Personal stories are used with permission or quoted from existing publications.

Too many friends to name individually have prayed for my inspiration and sometimes provided it in their own lives. I am so grateful for their encouragement.

I am grateful to the publisher Chris Hayes of Gilead Books for so readily accepting the manuscript. He has been very encouraging and supportive through the the final publication. Dona McCullagh's editing has been painstaking and sympathetic throughout. As ever, Gareth Jones has been unfailingly helpful with my computer problems by bringing his expertise to my rescue. Thank you all.

Above all, praise be to the God and Father of our Lord Jesus Christ who saw, and has shown, what he could do through the more painful patches of lives offered to him. This has included the difficult experiences of special people known to me as well as a few of my own. If some of the lessons learned enlighten and encourage anyone else, I will be deeply grateful.

Introduction

Pain is something that most people naturally shrink from, yet it acts as a helpful warning. Those who lose awareness of pain, such as victims of leprosy, develop scars from the cuts and burns they had not felt. Unless treatment arrives in time the affected parts will become grossly and conspicuously disfigured. Sufferers are then shunned. It can be dangerous not to feel pain.

There are different kinds of pain, less obvious than cuts and burns. Over many years of paediatric practice, I have observed another side to painful experiences. My heart used to sink when a developmentally delayed child came into my clinic, sometimes with combined physical and mental problems. I was saddened both by the family's great burden and by what little I could do to relieve it. Though this often remained the case, I began to see that along with their trouble many had found hidden treasure. Some of us will have found this to be true in our own lives. We do not (and neither should we) deliberately self-harm or hurt others for the sake of such possible gain. Pain usually arrives without invitation but, given support, it can in time have a creative effect. Families I cared for and many others have taught me this perspective.

It was evident at a glance that one boy I met was intellectually very much delayed. As his mother gave me permission to use his photograph in my talks she added, with some pride, 'When you use it, tell them that he brought a lot of love.' Another mother wrote of the warmth and affection she had found among families with a disabled member. Love, warmth and affection—these are invisible but very precious qualities that I had been overlooking in these special families. Many still do so. The discovery will be made in many other circumstances—by looking below the surface we can often detect unexpected treasures. Most of us tend to judge by outward appearances, yet, as even a quite young child once observed to me, 'It's not what people look like on the outside that's important. It's what's on the inside that matters.' Jesus commented that little children may see what the wise and learned miss (Matt. 11: 25).

That thought takes my mind back to the Old Testament story of a young shepherd boy, good looking but still with a lot to learn. His father presented him as a complete afterthought to the prophet on the lookout for a future king. Although David seemed an unlikely candidate, the divine verdict went deeper. His handsome brothers had seemed eligible enough 'but the Lord looks at the heart' (1 Sam. 16: 7). After many painful episodes, King David finally ascended to the throne and had a long and memorable reign. He became a notable ancestor of the Lord Jesus Christ.

In the varied experiences of our lives, however bad or painful things may seem to be, something good can slowly emerge from them. The more we look, the more unexpected examples we may find of this principle of gain from pain. It can be perceived through the small irritations of life as well as in greater trials. It can even emerge when someone, young or old, is dying or bereaved. Those still suffering may find this an insensitive, even offensive, conclusion.

Yet it is also the great message of the first Good Friday and Easter Sunday when Jesus' agonising crucifixion was followed first by his glorious resurrection, then his return to his Father and the gift of his Holy Spirit. That sequence continues to offer hope to any still carrying a heavy personal cross. Our Lord promises to comfort and relieve such burdens (Matt. 11: 28–30). In time we may look back in wonder as his creative purposes become clear. Like a mini-resurrection, we may gratefully discover the gift of new insights to use in his service, so adding to his glory.

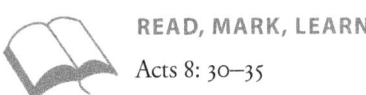

READ, MARK, LEARN

Acts 8: 30–35

Abbreviations

Biblical books abbreviated in the text, listed alphabetically:

1 Chron.	1 Chronicles
Col.	Colossians
1 Cor.	1 Corinthians
2 Cor.	2 Corinthians
Dan.	Daniel
Deut.	Deuteronomy
Eph.	Ephesians
Exod.	Exodus
Gal.	Galatians
Gen.	Genesis
Hab.	Habakkuk
Heb.	Hebrews
Isa.	Isaiah
Jer.	Jeremiah
Mal.	Malachi
Matt.	Matthew
Mic.	Micah
Phil.	Philippians
Prov.	Proverbs
Ps.	Psalms
Rev.	Revelation
Rom.	Romans
1 Sam.	1 Samuel
1 Thess.	1 Thessalonians
1 Tim.	1 Timothy
2 Tim.	2 Timothy

CHAPTER 1

Pain comes to us all

'OUCH! THAT really hurt!' Whatever the reason, most of us have said this at some time in our lives. Pain comes in different forms and with variable intensity. People vary, too, in their reactions to discomfort. Some are softies, others are stoics.

PHYSICAL PAIN

Bodily discomfort ranges from a pinprick to intense agony, dependant on the cause. If it is bad enough sufferers will seek medical aid and have to answer lots of questions. How long has this been going on? How would you describe the pain—stabbing, throbbing or aching, intermittent or constant? Where is it felt most and does it move from place to place? Where would you put it on a scale of one to ten? Does anything relieve it? The answers often suggest a likely diagnosis.

It is harder to elicit a clear story when the patient is a baby or small child. Body language may be suggestive, as when an infant's screams come and go, with legs drawn up at the same time. 'Wind' is not an adequate diagnosis for such colicky pain without excluding something more serious. An older child may clutch at an evidently painful and pink ear. Pain can be a (literal…) wake-up call, announcing that something is not right. Full examination and appropriate tests can confirm or cancel the tentative diagnosis initially suggested by the symptoms and signs.

What is certain is that the pain has been bad enough to make someone call for help and, in the developed world, help of different kinds is usually available. For some it will require the skills of a surgeon, who may temporarily cause a different kind of pain before relief and healing can follow. Whatever its cause, to seek and find help for physical pain is usually the way to eventual recovery. It can often be life-saving. Physical pain therefore has purpose. We should take note of the whimpers and investigate the shouts.

Probably the worst pain I have ever witnessed was long ago when as medical students we were taken to see an ashen-faced man who was thrashing about on his hospital bed in an open ward. He was clearly in physical agony. He had fallen from a roof and (at least) ruptured his spleen. We were shown that his abdomen was as rigid as a board, no doubt because of acute internal bleeding. Today he would have been rushed to an intensive care unit, probably scanned and transfused prior to urgent surgery. In those less advanced days it was far from certain whether he would ever reach the operating theatre, but he became the object of a never to be forgotten tutorial for a group of shocked young people. He died not long afterwards. His pain served only to bring him to hospital for help that was not forthcoming. This is still so for many of the world's poorest people.

EMOTIONAL PAIN

That man's physical agony was obviously associated with extreme emotional anguish and fear.

For less acute states, fear of what may have caused the pain, or anxiety about what may need to be done about it, can each intensify physical pain. A tense emotional state may follow crashed hopes or bereavements of many kinds. Living in a war zone with the constant threat of danger or even an unpleasant personal confrontation can set the pulse racing. Depending on the cause, such aroused emotions range from an inner rawness or numbness at one end of the scale, through agitated apprehension, to utter despair at the other. The onset of symptoms may be delayed, as in some cases of Post Traumatic Stress Disorder. Some people weather these onslaughts well but the anxiety level of others peaks so rapidly as to cause panic attacks, or plunges steeply into thoughts of trying to end it all. To talk through the feelings with an understanding friend or counsellor may enable swifter recovery.

For many, fear of dying takes over even when an illness is not actually life-threatening. When life expectancy is known to be genuinely limited, a variety of emotions arise. Classically there is a mixture of denial, bargaining, depression and an eventual coming to terms with the inevitable. I recall a teenager whose malignant tumour of the leg had required amputation. No-one had known how to break the news to her clearly enough, either of the diagnosis or the consequences of the planned surgery. The operation simply went ahead. She had not understood the full implications of someone's stumbling words until she woke up, minus the leg. She then turned her face to the wall in shocked denial of the reality.

What followed was a roller coaster ride through different emotional reactions: initially withdrawal and depression, later the choice of long skirts to hide her artificial leg. When she eventually realised that the disease was spreading she started glue-sniffing and drinking from the ward's bottle of bleach. Over these months the girl and her mother became alienated, neither knowing how to express their feelings to the other as she grew sicker. Family therapy helped and the youngster finally asked to go home on what turned out to be the day before she died. Her mother later reported that they had talked to each other as they had never talked before, adding, 'It was the best night of our lives'. As they each came to terms with the inevitable they were reconciled just in time.

A Christian youth leader, Nigel Lee, developed the same malignant disease in his leg as that teenager's. Older and wiser, he understood that it threatened his life. He commented to a friend, 'This is when people will get to see if I really believe what I have been preaching about'. He hobbled round the hospital ward sharing his faith with enthusiasm and humour. He was confident that he was on the way to meet his Lord and used an undoubtedly painful time to tell other patients how they could know the same joyful certainty as his by trusting that same Lord.

MENTAL PAIN
It is hard to separate mental from emotional pain but the former tends to be longer lasting or even a constant state of mind. It may be marked by agitation, confusion, multiple physical complaints, guilt, a sense of unreality or delusions of persecution. There is risk of turning to drugs or alcohol and subsequent addiction. After an initially elevated mood, melancholic or suicidal thoughts may follow. Should these lead to the act itself, a coroner will usually pronounce that the balance of the mind was disturbed.

Sufferers from mental illnesses such as schizophrenia, personality disorder or the autistic spectrum often lack insight, but suffer more should this sometimes break through. The only child of a couple I know was a beautiful young boy with serious attention deficit syndrome. His disruptive behaviour finally led to his expulsion from normal school to go to a special school designed for children like him. Sometimes he cried to his mother, 'Why am I like this? I don't want to be but I can't help it.'

SPIRITUAL PAIN

This kind of pain may go unrecognised. It includes a sense of helplessness when enduring severe pain of any kind with loss of hope that it will ever come to an end. People once confident in faith may decide that God has abandoned them in their suffering. The 'why me?' questions arise. Is God punishing them for past sins, remembered or forgotten? Matters are made worse when, like Job's comforters, others agree that this is so (Job 15: 4–6). Some supposed friends may also accuse sufferers of not having enough faith when prayers made for their healing seem to go unanswered. The idea that anything good can possibly come from the suffering is dismissed outright.

TOTAL PAIN

Physical, emotional, mental and spiritual pain can be experienced separately or together. This was so for a doctor friend of mine who developed a slowly advancing and life-threatening neurological disease. As time passed, she became increasingly unsteady, frequently stumbled and fell, her hands shaking uncontrollably. She lost her voice and swallowing often precipitated alarming episodes of choking. It seemed that the disease clouded her judgment, making her very fearful either that she would be admitted to hospital and kept alive on a machine, or that she would be buried alive.

Her training had forewarned her of the probable course of the illness. Accordingly, when still able to control her hands she had filled a syringe with drugs powerful enough to kill her. The first problem was that when she decided to use it her hands were too shaky to perform the injection. The other difficulty was that as a committed Christian she questioned the rightness of such an act. Spiritual turmoil was thus added to the rest. Although suffering their own anguish, neither her sympathetic husband nor the family doctor agreed to help with more than palliative care to relieve her symptoms. She resisted this for weeks, still hoping for the injection. All four kinds of pain came together for her.

THE SUPREME EXAMPLE

In his death, Jesus also experienced every possible kind of agonising pain, to be considered more in chapter 7. In his darkest hour, as he paid the penalty for human sin, he cried out, 'My God, my God, why have you forsaken me?' (Matt. 27: 46) As he died, he committed his spirit into his Father's hands and was raised from death on the third day following, later to be reunited with the Father in heaven (Acts 2: 32–33). Those who put their trust in his loving forgiveness will also pass through death to experience new life—an entrance, not a final exit (Phil. 1: 20–26). Meanwhile, in this present life they can be encouraged and strengthened in different ways through his promised Holy Spirit.

This was my doctor friend's experience. Her mini-crucifixion had tempted her to make a quick exit until she finally followed her Lord's example by committing her life into God's hands. His timing mattered much more than what she had planned for herself. In this acceptance came peace, helped by the delayed medication. Her family gathered round the bed, each giving her a final message in Scripture or song to encourage her spirit. By now unable to speak, she responded by blowing a kiss to each of them in turn. Somehow her husband managed to sing the Shepherd Psalm and as he finished she mouthed the words, 'for ever'—and gently died (Ps. 23: 6). How much better an end this was than if someone had found her body, killed by her own hand.

SPIRITUAL GAIN AFTER TOTAL PAIN

Some of these stories of other people's pain are hard to read, and were even harder for them to bear. It is my hope that together we shall see how, in God's hands, even experiences of deep despair can be eased, and not just by medical means. Our loving heavenly Father often mediates his spiritual support through the helping hands of others, to bring something positive out of what had seemed so negative. In so doing he encourages those being cared for and strengthens those who care for them (2 Cor. 1: 3–4).

Many sufferers know periods of painful questioning. At such times it can help to recall the triumphant outcome of Jesus' suffering on the cross. His relationship with the Father, though tested, finally held as God raised him up again. We do not need to wait to reach heaven before knowing the power of that resurrection even when experiencing the fellowship of sharing in his sufferings (Phil. 3: 10). Easy words? Yet they were written by a man who suffered more than most of us ever will (2 Cor. 11: 23b–29). I have also seen a dying woman, in great pain from the spread of cancer to her bones, say with a shining face, 'All I want to do is to glorify Jesus'. The awed reply was, 'That's what you are doing.' We are sometimes privileged to glimpse the reality of things unseen, even through our tears.

READ, MARK, LEARN
Psalm 42: 7
Psalm 22: 11
1 Corinthians 10: 11–13
Matthew 8: 5–7

BACKGROUND READING

Carswell, Roger, *Why me? Personal stories of hope in suffering* (Leyland: 10Publishing, revised edition 2016)

Mason, Mike, *The Gospel according to Job: an honest look at pain and doubt from the life of one who lost everything* (Wheaton, Illinois: Crossway Books, 1994)

Stott, John R. W., *The cross of Christ* (Leicester: InterVarsity Press, 20th anniversary edition 2006)

CHAPTER 2

Love's labour rewarded

TODAY I had two separate messages from a friend's delighted mother and sister that she had been safely delivered of her second child. I am reminded of Jesus' words about the pains of labour being forgotten in the joy of welcoming new life (John 16: 21). As one of a large human family, he had possibly joined in such celebrations after the births of James, Joseph, Judas, Simon and their young sisters (Mark 6: 3).

In many parts of today's world, as in Jesus' day, childbirth holds dangers for both mother and child. In general—and everywhere—more sympathy is expressed for the mother's labour pains than for the uncomfortable experience for the baby on the way. To hear the child's first cry brings a ripple of relief to all present, often with a tearful welcome from the happy parents. It is clear that the pains of labour have been productive. What about the discomforts infants go through before emerging to receive such a welcome?

ALL CHANGE

After months of floating in the dark in what is like a warm bath, cushioned from outside clamour and light, the baby starts to experience a gradually increasing constricting, expulsive force. After what can be many hours, he or she is squeezed, usually head first, through an uncomfortably narrow passage. Even though the soft bones of the infant skull are designed for easy moulding, this compression could well induce a headache. (An adult sometimes describes a migraine as 'like having my head in a vice' and so it could be for some babies during birth.) In the darkness of the womb the mother's heart can be heard going lub-dub with added tummy rumblings. At birth these are exchanged for the assault of the bright lights and loud sounds of a modern delivery suite. Sometimes the child suffers the indignity of being held upside down by the ankles, slapped, and even given an injection. No wonder new babies cry.

Before birth the movements of legs and arms have been restricted but now they can flail about in unaccustomed space. It must be such an enormous cultural shock to be born. Some thoughtful parents try to soften the impact by arranging for the delivery to be into a bath of tepid water, perhaps playing quiet music already made familiar before birth. Yet there is gain from the infant's expression of pain. Without that first big breath, independent existence would be impossible. It vitally modifies the circulation of the child's blood from that required before birth (when it is still linked with the mother's) to the different needs outside it. By opening up the lungs, crying changes the pressure in the heart and major blood vessels. When all goes well, the baby has a completely separate circulation. A satisfactory supply of oxygen now comes from breathing air, no longer dependant on the supply in the mother's blood.

WELCOME TO THE FAMILY

It is natural for new parents to want to comfort their crying baby. This is when we find other aspects of the Creator's careful design. When a distressed newborn infant is taken up to be calmed in the crook of the mother's left arm, the familiar soothing lub-dub may be heard again. By offering the child a variety of patterns to look at it has been found that the usual favourite is that of a face, especially the eyes. To be held in that position is also to be at the perfect focal distance for looking into the happy face of a parent. Crying stops as the new baby gazes attentively back into eyes filled with delight and, for now, unable to look anywhere else. Shock subsides in the security of loving arms instead of the earlier constricting wall of the womb. Babies still too small or sick to enjoy this experience will probably be in an incubator, but parents can hold their hands through the porthole and may sometimes establish eye contact.

If permitted, this quiet time of mutual appreciation is when many parents fall in love with their baby. Within days, infants repeatedly allowed to experience this will spontaneously fix their gaze on the most familiar face within a group, usually the mother's but fathers should not be left out. Babies are very ready to play their part in 'getting to know you'. This is something that parents need to understand but, especially overseas, have not always been encouraged to expect or play their part. God is three-in-one, Father, Son and Holy Spirit, and in this image we are created (Gen. 1: 27). Besides much else this must include that of loving inter-relatedness, for God *is* love (1 John 4: 8). The shared pains of childbirth are overcome by the joys of mutual affection.

This may shed new light on an oft-quoted statement by Jesus, 'You must be born again' (John 3: 7). He was referring to the spiritual rebirth that happens when we acknowledge that our wrong doing led to his agonising sacrifice as he took its penalty on himself. To accept his offer of forgiveness and a fresh, clean start is to be born into new and eternal spiritual life, committed to loving him as he first loved us. Jesus spoke of the even greater joy in heaven over this transaction than that experienced on earth when a new baby is born. New 'infants in Christ' (1 Cor. 3: 1–2) do not announce themselves with cries of pain but join in songs of praise (Luke 15: 7, 10), as they find a loving welcome. They are immediately adopted into a worldwide family, the family of the God and Father of our Lord Jesus Christ (John 1: 12–13).

GROWING UP

For the new family to stay close, relationships must be regularly nourished as they recover from the transient and largely unavoidable birth pangs. A chilling TV documentary recently told of an aristocratic couple whose shared lives were spent in relentlessly pursuing various forms of entertainment. Their three children were constantly left in the care of nannies and in later life lost all parental contact. The mother was asked if she now thought that she had been cold towards her children. She immediately replied, 'All my relationships are cold.'

A new family's bonds normally grow warmer as they enjoy time with each other. New additions to God's family similarly get to know him by spending time prayerfully learning from his word, illuminated by the Holy Spirit of Jesus. The Father's unfailing personal care nourishes the relationship. Nothing can happen to us that is beyond his loving control. Even so, like little children we are slow to be 'content whatever the circumstances,' (Phil. 4: 11–12) or doing everything 'without complaining or arguing.' (Phil. 2: 14). Experience teaches us that God's purposes are always good because he loves us. Spiritual infants are intended to grow up and become mature in him (Eph. 4: 13–15).

Dreaming about a baby is said to foretell the coming of a new idea. Be that as it may, I hope that the theme of this book will bring to birth new ideas for some who read it, and not only those about human parenting.

READ, MARK, LEARN

John 3: 7 1 Peter 2: 2
Luke 15: 7, 10 Ephesians 4: 12–15

BACKGROUND READING

Klaus, Marshall H. and John H. Kennell, *Maternal–infant bonding: the impact of early separation or loss on family development* (Saint Louis: The C. V. Mosby Company, 1976)

Mark Houghton, *Pregnancy and abortion: your choice* (Welwyn Garden City: Malcolm Down Publishing, 2017)

Parker, Russ, *Visions in the night: hearing God in your dreams* (London: SPCK, 2013)

CHAPTER 3

Not worth living—or of great value?

ACROSS THE world, when all goes well, the arrival of a new baby is usually a happy event. Yet there are still countries where the death rates for mother and child are much too high. Conversely, in the so-called developed world the same holds for the high level of mortality for unborn children whose parents have decided to abort them. Within weeks of conception, and as the result of certain routine tests, expectant parents may be told that there is something seriously amiss. There are abnormalities they should know about because, once delivered, their baby may face an early death or a longer life of disability. The idea is too often conveyed that such lives are of greatly diminished quality and not worth living.

Ending the pregnancy is all too easy, although a scan after five weeks' gestation would show a tiny beating heart, exciting and endearing when parents are allowed to look at it. Yet it can be hard for them to go against what sounds like wise professional judgment when floundering in the natural turmoil that unwelcome news must bring. Some parents have even chosen to abort babies with such a correctable defect as cleft palate. In one culture, a baby girl on the way could meet the same end if a scan showed an extra finger, for it would reduce her marriage prospects.

Dashed expectation is in itself a form of bereavement. Such parents need the support that would be offered for more obvious kinds of loss, but do not always find it. Advice by members of the extended family, and also some professionals, is frequently to get rid of the problem, that is, the baby-on-the-way. It is said that the quality of the child's life will be so impaired that it is best to bring it to an end. There is a move to liberalise the law but 24 weeks gestation is currently the legal cut-off point for most abortions in Britain. However, there is no legal limit on the disposal of babies with serious or life-threatening disabilities. They can be destroyed at any time before birth, with little or no follow-up offered to help the parents' subsequent sense of loss. They can feel relief, sadness and guilt all at once, even when it was by their own decision that they had lost their hoped-for child.

DOES QUALITY EQUAL VALUE?

Those who decide to go on with the pregnancy still need support, insight and courage. One obvious insight is to discriminate between *quality* and *value*. They are not necessarily the same thing, but can be treated as though they are. Antique ruins or historic flags, often of very poor quality, may be preserved as valuable national treasures. They are mourned when deliberately destroyed, for that little bit of history is now permanently lost. However disabled, the value of a human life lies in its being made in the image of God (Gen. 1: 27), a view not shared by those who do not know him. Apart from the years when his Son was incarnate, we know God as Spirit, not flesh. The imagery must therefore refer primarily to spiritual values, not physical attributes. These do not show up on scans, and need spiritual perception to recognise their important reality.

The apostle Paul wrote to the Colossians that Jesus was the image of his Father (Col. 1: 15). It was not his physique that made people marvel (Isa. 53: 2). His wonderful words impressed them and the authority with which he spoke (Matt. 7: 28–29) as did the great miracles he performed through the Holy Spirit (John 11: 43–45 and Acts 10: 38). He selflessly went about doing good and his Father publicly expressed his love for his Son (Matt. 3: 16–17). The love and closeness between the three members of the Trinity—Father, Son and Holy Spirit—is an important part of the imagery that should still hold, whatever a baby looks like.

A pale reflection of the divine image can be found in the natural interaction between new parents and babies. Extra sympathy and love are needed when there are special problems. Patience is needed, too, because such children often grow up to be much slower to respond and learn, or suffer other difficulties not easy to deal with.

It is likely that among the little ones taken up into the arms of Jesus to be blessed some were affected by physical or mental incapacities, or both. Perhaps that was why his disciples reacted by trying to make their mothers take them away (Matt. 19: 13–15). Similar hurtful attitudes can still hold. I was once in an English cathedral cafe in the company of a child with a grotesquely damaged face and eyes. A fellow diner asked her husband to change places with her so that she would not have to look at 'that child's awful face'. Happily, the little girl did not understand English, nor could she read body language, because she was blind.

HIDDEN TREASURE

The story of one special child was first told on the radio and later written up by her father. Millie was such a badly disabled baby that her parents were warned after the 20-week antenatal scan that she was suffering from severe brain malformation. They were offered an abortion. Instead they decided that their child was not a medical problem to be faced but a daughter, however imperfect, to be treasured and loved. Despite the many challenges that Millie brought with her, in the 20 months of her life she was truly valued by her parents and brothers. The family then found that, by not hiding her away, many others were drawn alongside to love her, too.

The realisation dawned that those who pour out love discover a God-given supply of more love to pour, because love comes from God. Her father wrote, 'There were many gains from sharing Millie in the church and community. We are still seeing the impact of her life…God called us to receive the gift of Millie for our lives…poured his love into her life and his love spilled over.' He concluded that God had taken something tragic and turned it into something beautiful, for love poured out is never wasted.

In a materialistic society it is sometimes argued that badly disabled children will contribute nothing to society. Instead, should they grow up, it is said that they will be a drain on the State's medical, social and educational resources. Future provision for them is viewed as not going to be cost-effective, an argument used to suggest terminating their lives. Yet Millie's is not the only story to make the point that their care is highly cost-effective in non-cash terms. Love poured out is often returned with interest. Surely in all societies that can only be of benefit to the whole community.

LOVE GROWS WHEREVER IT GOES

Broadcaster John Bell of Iona recently pointed out the number of times Jesus had healed people but sent them back to their communities rather than letting them stay with him. His blessings were given to be shared (Mark 5: 18–20 and Luke 5: 23–26). Even when physical and mental healing has not happened to their children, the miracle for many parents like Millie's has been a change in attitude, first in themselves and later in perceptive onlookers. What had at first looked like a tragedy brought with it a new capacity to give and receive self-giving love, first poured out and then replenished by the God who *is* love. This message needs to ripple out to those who air contrary views.

Like all other babies, whatever their problems, those with disabilities still enjoy being held close, quite unaware that some would have wished them dead.

The mother of one such child said, 'If he's not going to live I don't want to see him'. Although the baby was already dying, it was suggested, 'Maybe *he* would like to see *you*'. Later his mother was comforted by a photograph of her frail little boy looking up into her face as she held him. A few hours later, he died. This was not in the least unsympathetic to the parents' deep grief, but helped them to ease their child's short life and perhaps be comforted by that themselves.

PAST MISTAKES

At one time, in mistaken attempts to spare parents' suffering, midwives who delivered babies with serious deformity would either make sure that they did not breathe or hurry them away out of sight. Stillborn babies would also be quickly removed from the scene, though their parents had really needed the chance to say 'Goodbye' to them. In those unenlightened days it was considered too painful to let them see their babies, and no such opportunity was given. After experiencing this, one mother described repeated nightmares of searching for her child, in her dreams still living but lost. A second stillbirth followed but was more sympathetically dealt with, the staff encouraging her to hold, handle and take proper leave of her baby. There were no more nightmares and the story ended happily with a gleeful, 'Then God gave me twins!'

LONELY LIVES—OR A BETTER OPTION?

When such severely deformed infants survived birth, a number would be helped by corrective surgery. Where they could not be helped, the practice used to be to keep them in a side room, loving interaction denied them. Their parents might be given the unfeeling advice to 'go home and have another try'. Such babies sometimes died alone, the family notified by telephone. Many parents were left bitter and angry for years, feeling that they had failed their infants by not sweetening their brief lives. The tide turned when palliative and terminal care began to be applied to older children (chapter 5).

It was slowly realised that this approach could also help these special infants. They were not hospital property, and could be looked after in their own homes. Advice was still on hand from hospital staff familiar to the family, or a tuned-in general practitioner. Home care became the pattern for many babies born with *spina bifida** for whom surgery would have been futile, or even fatal. Few lived for more than a few weeks but their parents' reports later were significantly positive. Family relationships had become closer as they lovingly looked after their latest

---

* *Spina bifida* is caused by a fault in ante-natal development. Several vertebrae fail to close over the spinal canal, overlying soft tissues do not join up and the spinal cord is left dangerously near the surface. If not too extensive, the lesion can be closed surgically but some are too big to allow this or the infants too small and frail to survive it.

and weakest members. The babies, too, seemed contented in their care.

The lesson learned, it could be applied with benefit in other circumstances. The parents of one little fellow understood that his serious congenital bladder condition would allow him only a short life. Even so, they determined to make it as good as possible. They took him home, keeping in touch with the hospital staff who knew them. During his short life they took their son out and about, even to the zoo! He may not have felt much more than love and comfort but for a few weeks the young couple knew what it meant to be parents.

FOLLOWING A DIVINE PATTERN

Of course, the relationship to be longed for above all is for parents and children to enjoy a personal relationship with God through our Lord Jesus Christ. The pains of his crucifixion on Good Friday were endured with this in mind and his resurrection from the grave on Easter Day was God's seal of approval on the finished work (Acts 2: 22–24).

Time and again newness of life has been found in the midst of the grief caused by tragedy, including the birth, life and death of a disabled baby. In a small way, the cross and resurrection have been re-enacted in painful human experiences when entrusted to God's creative love. Jesus used the picture of a grain of wheat falling into the ground and dying before there can be a harvest (John 12: 24). Sometimes we have a glimpse of what this can mean.

FROM HURT TO HARVEST

Some years ago a baby was born in our local hospital with such severe *spina bifida* that he would not have been helped by surgery and may not even have survived it. This was in the days when it had been the practice for all such babies to be kept in hospital until they died. This little chap's ex-missionary parents never considered any other option than to take Tim home, where his mother would breastfeed him. I called to see how they were getting on and found such a loving atmosphere of peaceful acceptance in the home. It was clear that his parents had committed his short life into their heavenly Father's hands. He died a few weeks later.

Not long afterwards in our hospital another little boy, David, was born with the same condition and poor outlook. His parents, too, wanted to take him home so we introduced them to the first couple whose story encouraged them follow suit. These two families set a trend. Thereafter, most such infants went home and many died there. Sad as it was to lose a baby, there was satisfaction to the families in having given closer care in the home than would have been possible on a busy hospital ward. A whole departmental policy had been changed by the example of Christian parents whose self-giving love for their little boy was extended to help other families to do so too.

Some months later I discovered that something even greater had been happening. David had already died at home when his older sister was brought to see me. As we talked it became clear that this was another Christian family. 'We weren't believers when we had David,' said his mother. 'We went to church sometimes, so members of the congregation prayed for us when we had a disabled baby. That's how we be learned about becoming Christians.' Their baby was not the only one whose brief existence was used, under God, to make an eternal difference to others. Seventeen members of one family came to faith in the Lord Jesus after the birth and death of one of these special little people.

Not all families tell such stories. Many parents were left bitter and angry, especially those whose babies had been left behind in hospital without their care. There is more hope of good finally emerging from crashed hopes when the importance of committed relationships is recognised with loving support ready to hand. This is especially so when there is a desire to honour the divine image in each life, whatever the physical form.

Apart from birth injuries and genetic disorders, congenital deformities can follow exposure of the early foetus to certain known drugs, or a mother's excessive intake of alcohol. Antenatal infections such as rubella or the mosquito borne Zika virus can do great harm. So far, many disabilities have no explanation. Yet, when the pain is entrusted to our loving Lord and support given to the parents, we sometimes see how good may come from it. As with Millie's story, tragic circumstances can bring about a harvest of blessing.

The very idea can be rejected by frightened families, who will still need support whatever they decide to do. Without it they can remain angry and embittered for years, yet Millie, Tim, David and others have shown how, if our heavenly Father's help is accepted—usually mediated through other people—he is able to bring much gain, even out of such pain.

READ, MARK, LEARN
Mark 10: 13–16
Matthew 18: 19

BACKGROUND READING

Delight, Eileen and Janet Goodall, 'Love and loss: conversations with parents of babies with spina bifida managed without surgery, 1971–1981', *Developmental Medicine and Child Neurology* 32: August supplement no. 61 (1990): 1–58

Scott-Brown, Martin, 'Love poured out is never wasted', *Triple Helix* Summer (2013): 6–7

CHAPTER 4

Burdens can break or make

It is often said that a disabled child can put such a strain on the marriage that the parents split up. This can then be put forward as an argument for aborting such a baby on the way. Certain philosophers even promote it as rationalising early infanticide. No doubt for a couple to care for the very special needs of some of these children involves personal and financial strain, yet so it does to care for any young child. Each of them has special needs of some kind but most are considered well worth any cost involved. Public opinion tends to be biased in favour of what is generally viewed as normal. Those who betray this attitude, either verbally or non-verbally, add to the special burdens borne by parents of mentally and physically handicapped children.

THE IMPORTANCE OF SUPPORT
A comparative study tried to clarify the variable rates of parental divorce in different family circumstances. The

children either attended normal schools or those catering for special educational needs. The results produced some surprises. The parents of children in the special schools had no higher a divorce rate than the local average except for significantly socially deprived families whose children had moderate learning difficulties. As such parents were already under considerable economic stress the breakup could not be blamed entirely on problems with their children.

Families with physically disabled but normally intelligent children fared better, though a bigger survey would clarify this significance. The lowest rates of divorce were in families affected by cystic fibrosis, a condition where all the mucus in the body is very sticky. It noticeably affects secretions in the lungs and digestive tract, causing chronic chest infection, failure to digest nutrition properly and subsequently to thrive. Parents of these children usually share the daily burden of the child's intensive physiotherapy. They receive a great deal of support from a variety of advisers. The children are usually intelligent and learn to be co-operative.

It would be difficult to repeat such a study today when divorce, cohabitation and lone parenthood are commoner but it suggested that support is essential to sustain families burdened with disability, whether mental, physical or both. Not many socially deprived parents have the energy to set up a support group for children like theirs who have learning difficulties, though the schools they attend do what they can. Such help is generally on offer for more conspicuous and heart-rending forms of disability, such as Down's syndrome, cystic fibrosis, autism and more. Families with similar difficulties support each other in these groups as well as attracting public interest and raising funds. The way that the extended family rallies round is often striking, but can also be lacking. The major burden of care still falls on parents, most often on mothers when fathers are breadwinners.

ARE WE ALL IN THIS TOGETHER?

If we believe that we are made in the image of God we have already seen how this will impact on our relationships, for he is a threesome. In Christ he gave himself in sacrificial love to restore our broken relationship with the Father. His Spirit offers us help every day to do as the earthly Jesus did when he showed special concern for the sick, helpless, sad, downtrodden, poor and outcast. We are not all called to identical areas of need but it is likely that each of us could support somebody in at least one of those categories. If we offer our lives to God for this—sometimes sacrificial—service, he will guide us about how and whom to help. We may then be surprised to find an untapped well of love.

PRECIOUS TO GOD

As I write, it is 38 years this weekend since I was called to see Claire, a two-day-old baby girl who was convulsing. She was the first child of young and very worried parents,

Dick and Sarah. The convulsions were extremely difficult to control and in time it became clear that they arose from a serious neurological problem that would cause significant delay in all areas of her development. The first two years of her life were spent screaming or convulsing and despite their love for her, her parents became desperate and exhausted. Claire could still barely lift her head and they were not sure that she knew them. Was it time to follow the advice of others and send her into residential care? They could cope no longer.

In her book entitled *Precious to God*, Sarah describes what helped to resolve the question. She was introduced to a group of parents and children with similar problems who understood and helped each other. Claire was treated as a little person, not just a huge problem. She began to recognise and enjoy Dick and Sarah's company, and in turn they learned to interpret what she meant by her different sounds. Instead of crying at some of their overtures she would have a good giggle. Despite her limitations she was developing a distinct personality.

The other big change Sarah writes about was the realisation that God was with them and would help them to cope. This he did. As they demonstrated perseverance and humour despite the daily ongoing struggle, there was an impact on others for good. This was even more so when a second child, Jimmy, turned out to have the same problem as Claire's. Now there were two convulsing, giggling and developmentally delayed children to manage until Jimmy's death when two years old. His parents courageously said that Claire had trained them how to care for her little brother. The two children used to 'chat' to each other with contented noises and the occasional chortle until Jimmy died.

There had been a day when Sarah found it all too much. Exhausted from lack of sleep and the constant demands of the children, she left the house, calling to Dick, 'I'm leaving!' A moment later she heard their door slam followed by footsteps behind her. They were Dick's. He slipped his hand into hers, saying 'I'm coming with you'. They laughed at each other and went back indoors, their mood lightened ready to take up the burden again. Humour often saved the day, as when going out with both children in their wheelchairs, Sarah looked at Dick and said, 'We'll be taken for a couple of social workers from a home for handicapped children!' It was their buoyancy that spoke volumes to those who watched and wondered.

THE PEARL EFFECT

One of my favourite symbols is that of a pearl. Its origin lies within an oyster when a foreign body such as a piece of grit gets under its shell and becomes embedded in the creature's soft flesh.* It must be at least as painful as when a nail pokes up through the sole of a shoe. Slowly the rough grit

---

* For landlocked readers: an oyster is a bivalve mollusc that normally lives in seawater. It is considered a delicacy in seafood restaurants.

becomes coated with layers of mother-of-pearl, smoothing its surface and doubtless soothing the oyster's discomfort. Eventually a valuable pearl develops, much sought after by pearl divers and sold as jewellery. Something very painful has been changed into something very precious.

In response to this analogy, my brother remarked, as brothers do, that all this wasn't much help to the oyster. Giving up its pearl usually meant giving up its life...but when alive it must have found relief when the sharp surface of the grit was covered over. In any case, most analogies have a weak point! We may compare the mother-of-pearl to the comforting love of God, easing the pain as he gradually produces something precious.

The whole notion of a loving God can be determinedly scorned by those in pain, and indeed may only be recognised in retrospect by those who hesitantly believe. When his love is rejected, or support lacking, an abscess may form instead of a pearl. This can then throb away, causing chronic unhappiness, depression and resentment. The word of God, the Bible, is described as a two-edged sword (Heb. 4: 12). Here it may act as a therapeutic lance (Eph. 6: 17 and Isa. 66: 13). To receive its wise and encouraging words can eventually be to find consolation and healing (Isa. 43: 1–5a).

ABSCESSES, NOT PEARLS

Some of us might have met parents of disabled children who clearly resent the burden they carry with no notion of a loving, supportive God. If one partner blames the other for the problem, as with a genetically inherited disease, the whole family's relationships can become frayed, not strengthened, with associated depression and bitterness. An emotionally deprived youngster will pick up such vibes and respond with some kind of attention seeking.

PRUNING IS PRODUCTIVE

Keen gardeners know that in order to have a fine display of roses, the bush must be pruned ahead of time. Jesus said a similar thing about cutting off and burning up the dead branches of a vine in order to produce more fruit (John 15: 1–2). Sometimes life's experiences act in a similar way. What can feel like the cutting off of natural expectations can also be a pruning away of the dead ends of materialism and self-centredness. It could be an opportunity for producing more of the fruit of God's Spirit, namely patience and self-control as well as love, joy, peace, kindness, goodness, faithfulness and gentleness (Gal. 5: 22). We may sometimes glimpse these qualities developing in the lives of those who care for disabled youngsters. They do not speak of difficult children but of beloved children with difficulties.

THE EFFECT ON WITNESSES

Claire lived for eight and three-quarter years. At her funeral the little church was filled to capacity as she was remembered with affection. She had beamed a clear light into her parents' lives and enlightened those of many others. Good things had emerged out of all the pain, once again illustrating 'the pearl effect'. Some spoke of the impact for good made on them by her short life, together with appreciation of her parents' fortitude under their severe pruning. Addicts had dropped the habit, a broken marriage was restored and others were made to reassess their priorities. It had been made abundantly clear that lives spent in self-giving love were richer than those whose aim is self-pleasing.

I am reminded of the passage in the letter to the Hebrews about 'a great cloud of witnesses' who encourage us to 'run with perseverance the race marked out for us,' just as Jesus had done (Heb. 12: 1). Those who had been watching Dick and Sarah run their difficult marathon shared in their joy when a year after Claire's death a lovely baby girl, Alice, was born. As she grew up, she was made familiar with stories of Claire and Jimmy. There came a day when she overheard someone talking to Sarah, ignorant of the family history, and suggesting that it was time that she produced a brother or sister for her little girl. The child immediately and indignantly protested, 'I've already got a brother *and* a sister but they're both in heaven.' Out of the mouth of babes!

LONG-TERM NEED FOR SUPPORT

Until Sarah's untimely death, she and Dick remained my valued friends. Despite all their problems, or because of them, I have seen them grow in patience, love and deep understanding. There were undeniable strains on their marriage, including a time of painful separation years after the deaths of Jimmy and Claire, when Alice was a teenager. There can be unseen repercussions from long years of stress, and the need for support never ends. Many find it in a loving church family. Thankfully, just as a broken bone is made stronger as it mends, the rift between Dick and Sarah was repaired, leaving their partnership stronger, their love tried, tested and made more mature. They had the added joy of Alice's happy marriage and lovely little boys, now giving comfort to Dick in his sadness.

BEAUTY FOR ASHES

Like many of us, parents like these sometimes find that past lessons need occasional refreshment to encourage them to sustain trust in the faithfulness of God. Pain added to pain brings many questions but when trustfully handed over to him can be used productively, just as pruning results in greater fruitfulness. The wisdom acquired on the way is valued by many others when undergoing their own sadness and loss.

God does not waste experiences, good or not so good. When accepted and offered up into his loving hands he will sometimes use them to teach us lessons that will later be helpful to others. He takes the long view and his purposes are always for the best. All gratitude and honour are then due to him, for it is he who exchanges dead ashes for a crown of beauty (Isa. 61: 3).

 **READ, MARK, LEARN**
Matthew 13: 44–45
Luke 11: 46
Galatians 6: 2
Isaiah 61: 1–3
Matthew 11: 28–29

BACKGROUND READING

Bowen, Sarah, *Precious to God* (Crowborough, East Sussex: Christina Press, 1997)

Goodall, J. and P. W. Jones, 'Do disabled school children disable a marriage?', *Maternal and Child Health Journal* 13: 5 (1993): 151–59

CHAPTER 5

Entering the valley: scared or serene?

IN 1967, a remarkable woman opened a hospice in London for the care of people in the last stages of their final illness. Dr Cicely Saunders was triply qualified, first as a nurse, then as an almoner (today's hospital social worker) and finally as a medical doctor. For years she had been working hard towards this fulfilment of an earlier vision to provide good terminal and palliative care. In this she was inspired and encouraged by some of her dying patients.

When her dream became a reality, it was immediately clear that her establishment of the new St Christopher's Hospice met a felt need. Residents were helped to live as fully as they could until the end came, and not made to feel that death was imminent from the moment they came through the doors. Each symptom was treated with appropriate medication, not by a one-size-fits-all dose of painkiller or sedation. When relieved and relaxed, questions often surfaced and received gentle, honest answers. For a time, when circumstances allowed, some could take their treatment at home.

Families were involved as closely as possible, sometimes needing guidance about coping with difficult but precious conversations. Later they were offered support in their bereavement. All this was so different from the experience of dying on an acute ward in a busy hospital, primarily geared to making people better. There was then a sense of failure and embarrassment if instead they died. Hospice care normally offered something better, and the hospice movement grew.

DYING CHILDREN NEED HELP TOO

So far this kind of care had not been offered to families with dying children. In most cultures it is very hard for adults to accept that children may die. In the West we have become all too familiar with televised pictures of starving infants or the weeping families of war victims. We are shocked when a child is killed by an abusive relative or drunken driver. When a child's illness, dying and death come closer to home we get uneasy and don't know how to cope.

In the 1970s there came onto our paediatric team in Stoke-on-Trent a sensitive and competent Christian doctor named Jennifer Chapman. After she left us, Jennie first went to work with the leukaemic unit at London's Great Ormond Street Hospital for Sick Children. She followed this with an eye-opening experience at St Christopher's Hospice, working alongside Cicely Saunders. In the interval we had kept in touch and after these two placements Jennie signalled back to me that we were not giving children proper terminal care. Instead we could put them through all kinds of painful tests and treatments as we tried to cure the incurable. It is interesting to note in passing that in our late teens both Jennie and I learned that our mothers were dying of malignancy, no doubt tuning us in very personally to end-of-life pains and problems.

At first, I bridled at Jennie's suggestion that any local children under our care were not being treated appropriately. Then we looked carefully at the notes of the last little patient to die on our wards (of cystic fibrosis) and were shocked. Her repeated chest infections and persistent distressing cough needed several sessions of physiotherapy each day to shift a little of the sticky mucus. In addition, her poorly absorbed food had left her seriously underweight and lacking in stamina. Her record described a child clearly at an advanced stage of the disease. She was labouring for breath, even in an oxygen tent. The tent obstructed her parents' access to her and their visits were accordingly sparse and short. On one of these they had left the inappropriate gift of a colouring book on top of the tent, then gone home.

Gradually the chest infection got worse, the child was exhausted and although a series of doctors examined her, each prescribed a different antibiotic with no effect. Throughout all this, her notes made no mention of any discussion with her mother or father that their little girl was dying. Although her parents needed to know that there was no real hope of recovery we could still offer a different kind of care. Yet attempts at cure were still going on.

FIGHTING TO THE END OR EASING THE HOMEWARD RUN?

Doctors can be experts at denial, seeing death as failure on their part so keeping up the fight against it. This is particularly true of those on the front line, who are usually junior staff. It would have been appropriate at this stage for the parents to be helped to get closer to their child and to come to terms with her approaching death. Trying to cure must now yield to keeping her as comfortable as possible. A basic rule in paediatric care is that the patient is the whole family, not just the sick child. Hindsight showed up the neglect of this rule.

With Jennie's help we put together a similar plan to that used for dying adults at St Christopher's Hospice, offering careful attention to the physical, emotional and spiritual needs of both patient and family. We had not long to wait before putting the new plan into practice and the results were amazing. The second child, Rachel, was eight years old and had the same advanced disease as the first. As she neared her end, instead of persisting with forlorn attempts at cure when she was clearly dying, Rachel was given treatment to relieve the anxiety caused by her difficult breathing. Any futile or intrusive therapy was stopped.

On her last day, Rachel spoke to her Christian parents about hearing singing. She looked beyond them with such evident delight that they asked who she could see. 'Jesus' she replied. A little later she struggled out of bed to give a hug to each parent in turn as they sat either side of her, then died in her father's arms. What more evidence did we need that palliative care was the treatment to offer when decline was irreversible! Dying children need help, too. Jennie and I used that as the title for our first joint paper when we wrote up the two stories in *The British Medical Journal* (1979).

There followed several more papers on this important but previously neglected subject, and sadly (but productively) more opportunities to practise it. We did not always get it right, but it gradually became clearer about when it was time to focus on the relief of symptoms instead of working for cure. A team approach paid off as comments from nurses can be so helpful, for they are much closer to their young patients, both literally as nurses and quite often in age. Together we learned to do better.

CHILDREN VARY IN THEIR UNDERSTANDING OF DEATH

In their early years the minds of sick or dying young children cannot anticipate the course of their illness. They learn on the basis of a shared (matching) experience, such as attendance at a hospital clinic with other children they get to know there. Those of normal intelligence observe what is happening to others and tend to apply this to their own condition. Understanding is sharpened when parents are obviously anxious or tearful. It helps when they manage to explain in terms familiar to the child why they are so upset. What they find painful to do dispels their children's confusion, to mutual gain.

Marc was the five-year-old friend of David, a boy who had died of leukaemia after the boys had for some time attended the same clinic. Marc missed his friend and may also have overheard adult conversation, as small people tend to do. Out of the blue he first asked his mother, 'Is it going to happen to me like it happened to David?' That was followed with, 'Am I going to die, Mum?' His startled mother understandably said 'No' to the first question but then regretted being untruthful so said 'Yes' to the second. Sensibly (or inspired) she added, 'You'll probably die before Mum and Dad but we'll be with you when it happens. In any case, it's not going to be today.' That was enough to satisfy a mind that could not yet think far ahead in abstract terms but was content to be assured that relationships with his family would hold for as long as he needed them.

Marc's four-year-old sister could see how her brother was no longer able get up and play, and was becoming more and more unwell. At that age she could look no further ahead, so to have his tiredness pointed out to her was enough information for now. The older sister needed a fuller explanation of his illness, its effects and likely conclusion. The family had moved house a few times so this made a good matching analogy. Marc's body was like his house and as his legs became paralysed the house was starting to fall down. The older sister understood the added abstract implication that after he had left his familiar house, just as they had gone to live somewhere else, her brother would go on to 'the house of the Lord', in heaven (Ps. 23: 6). That would be so lovely that he would never need to move house again.

It is several years before a young child grasps the idea that death is a permanent state. After a simple explanation of what will happen, going to the funeral can be instructive and helps children to feel included in saying that final 'Goodbye'. It needs to be made clear, though, that a dead body will not feel lonely, cold or frightened in the earth, or feel anything at all even in the flames. The greatest pain afterwards will be to miss the dead person but, lovingly handled, the experience can become a growth point in understanding for young minds—gain even, from such deep pain. Naturally, adults find such an approach hard but the benefits are great.

INSPIRED MINDS THINK ALIKE

The book of Genesis begins with a comment that the Spirit of God was hovering before the creation of our world (Gen. 1: 2). It seems that he still broods to bring to light and life innovative ideas of which he is the source (Col. 1: 9). As he is also the God of all comfort, it is not surprising that he inspires ways of giving comfort to those who mourn, bringing gain to their loss (2 Cor. 1: 3–4). What is perhaps more surprising is that he inspires different minds in different places with the same ideas at the same time.

Hospice care for adults was already established when, in 1982, Helen House—the first children's hospice—was opened in Oxford. Others were at last learning how to ease the last stages of a dying child's life. Before that many futile fights had been fought, causing more pain in the process of trying to save lives. We were encouraged to find that our own new practice was in line with that of Oxford's more prestigious centre.

The original Helen was a little girl with a serious, advancing neurological condition, mentally and physically disabling. The family was known to the then Mother (now Sister) Frances Dominica of the local All Saints Sisters of the Poor convent in Oxford. As the child's care was exhausting her loving parents, it seemed natural to their friend Frances to give them a break by having Helen to stay with her for a weekend. The visits became more frequent and from that the idea for Helen House was born. Separate accommodation for teenagers was provided later, so it is now known as Helen and Douglas House.

A PAINFUL PROBLEM BECOMES PRODUCTIVE

At one time many professionals found that facing up to the needs of a dying child was too painful to bear. The personal needs of that child and others in the family were neglected, and children were not given an explanation about what was happening. In truth, many parents did not really understand either. Brothers and sisters could even be sent away, making them feel punished for whatever it was they had unwittingly done to cause the illness. Meanwhile the young patient endured aggressive and unpleasant therapy to the very end, possibly feeling punished, too. It is not difficult for young minds to find a small transgression to blame for such inappropriately huge consequences. A well-developed sense of proportion takes years to develop.

Slowly medical professionals began to tune in to these more personal aspects of paediatric care. Parents needed to be informed of the likely course of an illness. Nurses and doctors had to learn how children of different ages think, enabling them to advise others on answering children's questions, spoken or unspoken. Simple explanations should be appropriate to the children's ages. Both sick and well children need at least to know that they are caught up in illness, not punishment, and that they will always be loved. Siblings sometimes have old quarrels that need to be put to rest before it is too late.

Quiet conversation between family members can be so precious at such times. This is particularly so when the whole family is supported by faith in a living, loving Lord Jesus. The one who in his earthly life so clearly loved and blessed little children can be trusted to take care of the dying child, and those who will be left behind.

Hospitals tend to be busy places concentrating on cure, but it is not impossible to practise proper terminal care on a ward. The idea of hospices for children has spread from the first Helen House in Oxford to many other parts of the UK, as well as overseas. They offer palliative, terminal and intermittent respite care whilst specialist nurses may deliver hospice type care in the home. For less experienced carers, advice is only a phone call away.

All these developments are traceable to a selfless act of costly commitment by an inspired woman, Frances, who was ready to set self aside in order to share and bear someone else's burden (Gal. 6: 2). By now countless families have gained from that first thoughtful burden-bearing, including the many young people who have been helped to live whilst dying.

READ, MARK, LEARN

Jeremiah 17: 14
Psalm 23: 4
2 Corinthians 12: 9
Philippians 1: 20–21
Revelation 21: 4
1 Thessalonians 4: 13–14

BACKGROUND READING

Chapman, Jennifer A. and Janet Goodall, 'Dying children need help too', *The British Medical Journal* 1, no. 6163 (1979): 593–94

Dominica, Frances, *Just my reflection: helping parents to do things their way when their child dies* (London: Darton, Longman and Todd, 1987)

Goodall, Janet, *Children and grieving* (London: Scripture Union, 2nd edition 1999)

Hill, Lenore (ed.), *Caring for dying children and their families* (London: Chapman and Hall, 1994)

Wyatt, John, *Dying well* (London: InterVarsity Press, 2018)

CHAPTER 6

The paradox of pain:
If God is almighty, why does he allow it?

A SMALL BOY was studying with interest a spider's web when a fly flew into it and was immediately seized and stored by the spider in residence. 'Mummy,' said the child, 'is it true that God is love?' His mother, who had not been looking, replied 'Yes, darling, it's true.' She was pleased that her little son was evidently thinking over the verse he had learned at his Bible class. The next question came, 'And does he know that spiders eat flies?' Despite sensing a hazard ahead, the mother pressed on with her instruction, 'Yes, Billy, God knows everything. He knows all about spiders and flies because he made them.' The wobbly landed. 'So doesn't he *mind?*'

The paradox of pain is still a puzzle to much older minds than Billy's, especially in the context of human suffering. Believers in an almighty creator God find it hard to reconcile his supposedly loving omnipotence with the reality of so much pain in the world. If he is so powerful, why doesn't he put a stop to it? Cries of 'It's not fair' also suggest divine injustice.

Those who do not believe in God frequently cite suffering as the main reason for their disbelief. Theologians also grapple with the problem. Their arguments can be less appealing to doubters than it is to meet sufferers who still trust in the loving purposes of God. The paradox of pain cannot be neatly solved by reasoning it out like a crossword puzzle, with its interaction of vertical and horizontal clues. For unaided human intellects, it remains an unfathomable mystery.

As the apostle Paul wrote of this mystery, he was not speaking with superior wisdom (clever though he was) but with insights given by the Holy Spirit, 'so that your faith might not rest on human wisdom, but on God's power' (1 Cor. 2: 4–5). I recall taking a young doctor to visit Nigel, a teenager dying at home of lung cancer. The boy had recently put his trust in God and was wonderfully at peace. So far, the doctor's training had been based on organic medical wisdom, and he found this atmosphere 'unnatural'. He needed to learn that it was actually supernatural, a glimpse of God's sustaining power made perfect in weakness.

WHY, LORD?

However bravely individuals face their pain and suffering, we (and they) may still ask, 'Why, Lord? Why do you let this sort of thing happen? Don't you *mind?*' Some who read this may be asking that question just now, either on their own behalf or concerned for someone else. Suffering has broken into their lives and the pain of it is awful. It must not be trivialised. I have hesitated to probe into this difficult subject for fear of coming up with unhelpfully slick or dubious answers. When people suffer severe pain, God alone knows his purpose for the final outcome. I can only share a few reflections.

We can be sure of some things God does *not* always mean by allowing pain. Some sufferers mistakenly think that pain is invariably punishment for past sins, remembered or forgotten. The book of Job starts with a glimpse of his blameless, upright and happy life before God gave permission to Satan to test his faith. For a long time, Job then experienced various kinds of suffering, including his friends' lack of sympathy. Like him, some whose pain persists despite earnest prayer may find themselves accused by others of undisclosed sin, or of not having enough faith to be healed. This only adds pain to pain.

Job himself was greatly mystified as to why all these calamities were happening to him. In the end God put his troubles into perspective with an overwhelming review of his divine creativity, power and authority. Clearly, such a mighty God could easily have intervened to relieve him, so must have held back for a very good reason. Job was encouraged to keep trusting him and God abundantly restored his faithful servant's health and prosperity. Of course, a new family could not replace the never-to-be-forgotten dead children. Sensitive scars would remain.

Scripture tells us that God does indeed sometimes act to discipline and even punish his errant people, following flagrant acts of disobedience or hypocrisy (2 Kings 17: 14–20 and Acts 5: 1–11). We are assured that to recognise, repent of and confess the sin is to find that God is faithful and just to forgive us. He will restore the damaged relationship (1 John 1: 9). Our part is to trust him completely in what he allows.

Whatever the circumstances, many people dismiss outright the idea that anything good can come out of suffering, despite the assurance of Scripture that *in all things* God works for the good of those who love him (Rom. 8: 28).

PAINFULLY OPPOSED VIEWS

Before exploring how pain first entered human experience, we need to digress a little. Christians disagree as to whether the creation story at the beginning of Genesis should be taken literally or figuratively. In his *NIV Bible Handbook* (2014), Christian theologian Alister McGrath, Professor of Science and Religion at the University of Oxford, suggests that the author of Genesis 1 is not answering the question 'How?' He is instead encouraging us to say 'Wow!', exclaiming in wonder at God's mighty works, crowned by the creation of human beings in his own image (p. 3). Genesis chapter 1 is not a scientific explanation of the origins of the universe but an introduction to the work of its wonderful Creator.

Others have written more about how the sad and painful alienation of science and religion first came about. Much insight would be gained if each side learned from the other. God is the greatest scientist of all and is graciously revealing ever more of his wonders to those exploring them, whether or not they acknowledge his handiwork.

THE SOURCE OF PAIN

If we simply look at the story as it stands, there are important lessons to learn. Early on in Genesis we meet Adam and his wife Eve, both made in God's image. In the beautiful Garden of Eden they evidently enjoyed a close relationship with him and with each other. God had declared all of his creation to be very good, so would have formed human beings with a fully intact nervous system, complete with fibres to conduct pain. They would also have been given the capacity for moral reasoning, aesthetic enjoyment and, importantly, the exercise of self will with its freedom to make choices. Sensations of pain probably lay dormant as Adam and Eve walked at ease with their Creator.

THE FALL

The third chapter of Genesis explains how suffering arrived and destroyed this idyll. God had given clear instructions to Adam, who would no doubt tell them to Eve. Their freedom was limited. On pain of death they were forbidden to eat fruit from a particular tree in the garden, the tree of the knowledge of good and evil. So far, they had only known God's goodness. It was evidently Satan, slippery as a serpent, who told Eve that God's warning was a lie.

Eating the forbidden fruit, he said, would give access to God's hidden wisdom and knowledge.

Eve was tempted. She saw how attractive the fruit looked, liked what she saw, craved a taste, took, ate and shared it with Adam. By ignoring God's warning, her headlong sequence set the pattern for all time. The path that ends in falling into temptation remains the same. First to look, to like the look, to desire the likeable object (person or situation) and take it—what a familiar route this is, often influencing someone else to fall too, with unforeseen and painful consequences.

The possibility of harmony between a holy God and mankind is anathema to the enemy of our souls. His first attempt to destroy it was so successful that God had to send the disobedient pair out of Eden lest they succumb to something worse. They had not specifically been barred from enjoying fruit from the tree of life, but to eat it would make them immortal. This was acceptable when they lived in harmony with their Creator but was not to be contemplated in their present fallen state. They had defaced his image in them and, no longer to be trusted, must be banished from his companionship and out of the garden (Isa. 59: 2). As foretold, the price of wilfully disobeying God was eventual death. This landmark event became known as the Fall.

THE FAR-REACHING CONSEQUENCES OF DISOBEDIENCE

Immediately everything changed. Pain was a new experience. When shame and guilt had made them hide away from their

Lord, Adam and Eve knew emotional and spiritual pain. The worst thing to bear would be broken harmony with him and shattered trust in each other. In the wild world outside the Garden of Eden, Adam would experience the physical pain of aching muscles after laboriously clearing away prickly thorns and thistles. Eve would discover the pains of her own hard labour when she gave birth to baby Cain. The dormant sensations of pain in all its variety were aroused in them both following their outright disobedience. Their descendants would carry the same bias to self-will and suffer for it (Rom. 5: 12).

The first taste of that desirable fruit opened the eyes of the guilty couple to realise that, unlike the animals around them, they were quite naked. With new knowledge of good and evil but without their earlier innocence they felt embarrassed to be seen uncovered, both by their seeking Lord and even by each other. Evil lies in the abuse of nakedness, not in the state itself. This was an early example of the muddled thinking that develops in minds out of touch with the wisdom of God.

FOOD FOR THOUGHT FOR SCEPTICS

There may be some reading the account so far who think that in itself it illustrates muddled thinking. They belittle the opinions of people who believe in God or claim that he speaks through the Bible. Scoffers certainly do not believe in the devil and his power to deceive. Even so, the critics can surely see at least one important point in the story as given.

Much of the world's suffering begins with unbridled self-centredness. (A believer would add, 'instead of obedience to God'.) The letter 'I' lies at the centre of the two words *sin* and *pride*. From the beginning, mankind's individual and communal capital 'I' has caused endless problems. Plain to see is the universal desire for selfish gain, whether of other people's territory, property or persons, and the greed of those with more than enough who ignore the plight of millions with too little. Except when it follows personal over-indulgence in food, alcohol, drugs or casual sex, many are justified in blaming someone else for their pain.

The natural world does not escape human neglect, as with the chain effects of deforestation or global warming. Some lovely animals, birds and insects face extinction because big business is affecting their habitat. A shrinking population of honey bees means inadequate pollination and smaller harvests of crops essential for life. Many if not most people give minimal respect to both the Creator and his creation.

The most ardent rationalist should see that, directly or indirectly, much of the world's suffering is caused by human selfishness. Whence this sense of right and wrong? Who sets the inbuilt standard of care so often ignored? Could it, after all, be God?

GOD'S ALMIGHTY POWER IS REVEALED IN WHAT HE HAS MADE

Those who dismiss the Bible as being God's word are invited to look at the created world (his 'other book') for evidence of a superb power at work (Ps. 19: 1–6). Studies ranging from embryology to space exploration speak of design both intricately detailed and overwhelmingly grand, yet many brilliant human minds continue to deny the probability of an imaginative and creative designer. Some are humble enough to acknowledge that such an awesome universe must have had a first cause. A few recognise this to be God, Creator of all.

Natural history programmes can surprise us. Nothing is too big or too small to suggest the work of a creative mind. Whether or not we know the scientific explanation, our spirits are lifted by a beautiful sunset or brilliant autumn colours. Marvels on the grand scale are complemented by closer appeals to our senses. We listen to a robin's joyful song (whatever it says to other robins). We admire the shiny petals of a buttercup, feel the softness of a lamb's fleecy coat or savour a whiff of perfume from a spray of honeysuckle. Even the perfection of a newborn baby's finger nails is more than would be needed for function alone.

It seems that a skilful artist has been at work in a gallery freely open to the public at all hours. It must be hard to believe that our wonderful, orderly and beautiful universe has had no superb intelligence at work, creating and sustaining it. Many believe there is no 'if' in acknowledging that God is indeed almighty. The pains of the world are well known to him, yet still allowed.

THE FALL AFFECTED MORE THAN HUMANS

The whole of creation was involved in the Fall (Rom. 8: 22). Afterwards the natural world, previously declared so good by the Creator, would now present new hazards, including death and decay. In his mercy God had clothed the naked couple with the protective skins of slaughtered beasts (the first deaths on record.) Adam had originally named these animals, so their killing must have shocked and grieved him. Now that death was on the agenda, so were threats to survival for vulnerable animals and plants. Without access to the plentiful greenery previously provided (Gen. 1: 30), some hungry creatures would doubtless become predators.

Yet the Creator did not abandon his fallen creation and his power still holds it together (Col. 1: 15–17). The ultimate gain after all these pains will be the coming of Christ's peaceful kingdom. Predators and prey will then lie down together—and lions will become grass-eaters! (Isa. 11: 1–2, 6–9)

JUSTICE AND MERCY

Many Bible passages tell of God's almighty justice and his merciful love. For those in the midst of painful experiences these two attributes, justice and mercy, may seem to be at odds with each other. Like the resolution of the crossword puzzle, it is as the vertical and horizontal clues connect that the conundrum starts to resolve. The solution to the problem of pain does not come through an intellectual brainstorm, as with the puzzle, but by finding the connection between Almighty God and the 'cross-work' he shares with his Son, Jesus Christ.

In the next chapter we'll look at what happens when the descent of holy justice meets the widespread arms of divine mercy. Many dilemmas resolve when, instead of two different views being held in conflict, they are found to form a creative relationship. Yet such resolution is likely to involve a unique and costly price-tag.

READ, MARK, LEARN

Psalm 19: 1 Romans 3: 10–12
Genesis 3: 22–23 Isaiah 12: 1–2
Isaiah 59: 2

BACKGROUND READING

Hindson, James, *Consider the lilies: Christians and creation care* (Malton: Gideon Books Publishing, 2016)

Kandiah, Krish, *Paradoxology: Why Christianity was never meant to be simple* (London: Hodder & Stoughton, 2015)

Keller, Timothy, *The reason for God: belief in an age of scepticism* (London: Hodder & Stoughton, 2009)

Lewis, C. S., *The problem of pain* (London, Glasgow and Hanley: Harper-Collins, 2015)

MacKay, Donald M., *The clockwork image: a Christian perspective on science* (Leicester: InterVarsity Press, 1997)

Mason, Mike, *The Gospel according to Job: an honest look at pain and doubt from the life of one who lost everything* (Wheaton, Illinois: Crossway Books, 1994)

May, Peter, *The search for God and the path to persuasion* (Welwyn Garden City: Malcolm Down Publishing, 2016)

McGrath, Alister, *NIV Bible Handbook* (London: Hodder & Stoughton, 2014)

Roseveare, Helen, *Living faith: Willing to be stirred as a pot of paint* (Tain, Ross-shire: Christian Focus Publications, 2016)

CHAPTER 7

The paradox of pain:
If God is love, how can he bear it?

YEARS AGO, shortly after its host country had opened up to the West, I visited an Eastern European institution. Recent photographs had appalled the outside world and the place I went to was typical. Infants housed there had wizened little faces with the unresponsive, staring eyes of severe emotional and physical deprivation. Many were dying. If not already orphaned, some had parents too poverty stricken even to visit. The children must have felt as abandoned as they looked.

A year or so later I was able to visit the same unit again. What a transformation! An American physiotherapist had left her comfortable home to spend long hours in that miserable place at her own cost. She devoted herself to stimulating the children with tender loving care. Some of the infants I'd met before were chubbier, smiling and eager to make eye contact. They were at last loved, responding with delight to the one who had saved them. It was all a work of grace, grace to the graceless, freely shown to bring them back to the land of the living.

GRACE AS UNDESERVED FAVOUR

The change brought about in those poor abandoned children reminded me of the transforming grace and love of our Lord Jesus Christ. Though he was rich he left his heavenly home and became poor so that we could be enriched by that grace (2 Cor. 8: 9). For 33 years he chose to mix with social outcasts, religious bigots and a few uncertain followers. Unlike the parents whose infants were left so bereft, our Father God had not deserted his children; it was their own self-will that alienated them from him. Their souls were shrivelled and dying until Jesus came. His gracious and costly sacrifice for the sins of the world brought the offer of forgiveness and the gift of eternal life for those who believe in him (John 3: 16).

GOD'S LOVE EXPRESSED THROUGH HIS SON

At the time of the Fall, God had warned the devil that one of Eve's offspring would one day 'crush his head', though bruising the heel that did so. It was many centuries before this was fulfilled when God's Son, the Lord Jesus Christ, was born into our world. In the early chapters of their gospels, Matthew and Luke tell the full story. I'll quote from some important verses in other books of the Bible, for ready reference. A basic truth is that 'God is love' (1 John 4: 16). Human suffering cannot quench that self-giving love. Instead our almighty God is full of compassion for sinners and sufferers even when they may think otherwise.

When Jesus, Son of God, was born to Mary, a virgin, the persons of God and man were uniquely combined. The apostle Paul described this as a mystery: 'For in Christ all the fullness of the Deity lives in bodily form' (Col. 2: 9). Throughout his earthly life Jesus witnessed the suffering of his people and, as Son of God, frequently and miraculously relieved it. Despite his deity, he would suffer human agony on the cross.

WHY JESUS WENT TO THE CROSS

When public figures are accused of some misdemeanour, they frequently deny any wrongdoing. Whether or not guilty as charged, they are not completely innocent, for 'all have sinned and fall short of the glory of God' (Rom. 3: 23). Just as in earthly courts wrongdoing carries a penalty, so sin is an offence against our Creator and brings God's judgment, 'For the wages of sin is death…' (Rom. 6: 23). Physical death has been experienced since the Fall but the spiritual death referred to is even more fearful. Satan loves to hold people 'in slavery by their fear of death' (Heb. 2: 14–15). Yet Paul's challenging verse continues, '…but the gift of God is eternal life in Christ Jesus our Lord' (Rom. 6: 23). When accepted, this love gift from Father and Son cancels the deserved sentence of spiritual death and dispels that fear.

COSTLY COMMITMENT TO RESTORED RELATIONSHIPS

Repairing mankind's broken relationship with God, and bringing life instead of death, could not be achieved without cost. The sinless Jesus paid that incalculable price on our behalf. 'God made him who had no sin to be sin for us, so that in him we might become the righteousness of God' (2 Cor. 5: 21). His whole purpose in coming into our world was to make us right with God by removing the barrier of sin between us.

To be made sin was the greatest of Jesus' pains, even worse than the physical and mental agony of a humiliating public crucifixion before a hostile crowd. He was taking upon himself the sins of the world and in exchange offering his own blameless goodness ('the righteousness of God') to those who accept his offer. It was an act of selfless love and grace. As the ordeal began and ended, Jesus spoke trustfully and confidently to his Father (Luke 23: 34, 46). Yet, in between, there had been hours of darkness when he asked why God had forsaken him. How so?

We are told that God's utter holiness is such that his eyes 'are too pure to look on evil' (Hab. 1: 13a). When his beloved Son was immersed under such a load of sin, it seems that the Father could not bear to look. Until the full price had been paid Jesus hung on the cross in deep darkness, literal and spiritual. It was in this time of dereliction that the sin he carried evidently made the same barrier between them as had come between God and disobedient mankind. He must have felt abandoned, no longer referring to 'Father' when he cried out that agonised question, 'My God, my God, why have you forsaken me?' (Matt. 27: 46). When suffering great physical or mental pain some are tempted to echo that cry. Yet no agony can ever match his, and neither can anyone else enter into our suffering with such sympathy and compassion.

At the time of that awful cry, Jesus and his Father, two members of the Trinity, were evidently experiencing a threatened rift in the closest, most loving and selfless relationship ever known. We forget that in this the Father must have suffered greatly as well as his Son. For a time, their previously unbroken unity was being agonisingly torn apart. Some theologians deny that almighty God can suffer, speaking of the 'impassivity' of God. Yet love can suffer, and he *is* love. Others find it hard to believe that the Father could look away from his Son in his darkest hour. We need to keep a reverent distance but I am persuaded to accept the implication of that terrible cry. With it, Jesus expressed how forsaken he must have felt. A distressed child may well feel deserted when wheeled alone into an operating theatre and approached by oddly dressed strangers. Parents may partially identify with their child's feelings but (usually) have to wait anxiously outside. They have not ceased to love the little one but know that the surgery must proceed without them whilst expecting eventual reunion and recovery. Perhaps this hints at what was involved for Father and Son as that greatest of all operations took place. Each of them suffered as the sin-sickness of the world, loaded onto Jesus, was exchanged for the offer of everlasting life instead of death. To repent and take up that offer is to be forgiven. The burden of our sin was included and has now rolled away, so we must never let ourselves pick it up again (Gal. 5: 1). We are completely forgiven!

Shortly before his arrest Jesus had said to his Father, 'I have brought you glory on earth by finishing the work you gave me to do' (John 17: 4). He died with the triumphant cry 'It is finished' (John 19: 30). He had completed his task perfectly, entirely innocent of personal sin and in harmony with his Father's will. Such love!—Son for Father, Father for Son, and all for us.

JESUS' RESURRECTION

On the third day following his Son's death, God raised him back to life. As the apostle Paul explained, 'He was delivered over to death for our sins and was raised to life for our justification' (Rom. 4: 25). Jesus' death would save believers from their sins; his return to life meant that God justified them, 'just-as-if' they had never sinned. Later he would receive his Son back to his side and later still the third member of the Trinity, the Holy Spirit, would be granted to his followers (Acts 2: 1–4).

The wonderful offer of eternal life is made to all who believe and accept it. Believers will escape the eternal death intended by Satan. Through the work of the Holy Spirit, peace follows the repair of their broken relationship with God (Rom. 8: 1, 5–7). That is how things were meant to be from the beginning. Amazingly we are also offered divine power, the same as 'he exerted when he raised him from the dead and seated him at his right hand in the heavenly places, far above all rule and authority, power and dominion, and every name that is invoked, not only in the present age but also in the one to come' (Eph. 1: 19–21). As we experience that same amazing strength we gradually learn to live God's way.

Although the devil's fate was sealed at the cross, he and his minions will continue rear-guard activities against us until their final destruction (Rev. 20: 10). Yet they can never undo the grace in which we now stand through the saving work of our Lord Jesus Christ (Rom. 5: 1–2).

FATHER AND SON WERE IN THIS TOGETHER

Jesus' death was his choice. Foreseeing his execution, he had said, 'The reason my Father loves me is that I lay down my life—only to take it up again. No one takes it from me, but I lay it down of my own accord. I have authority to lay it down and authority to take it up again' (John 10: 17–18). This authority had been given by his Father, about whom he also said, 'I always do what pleases him' (John 8: 29). This was a shared agreement *and* a shared action, made entirely out of gracious and undeserved love. There is no place at all for the caricature sometimes drawn of a sadistic father arranging the brutal sacrifice of his only son to pay for sins he had not committed. Others suggest that God, being perfect, could not suffer. Yet, made in his image, we are able to suffer with other sufferers, so surely the Father could not remain impassive at Calvary.

Exactly because God is totally almighty, he could readily have intervened and released his suffering Son from the cross. Our Lord Jesus Christ, God-made-man, restrained his own power (Matt. 26: 52–53). He 'did not consider equality with God something to be used for his own advantage: rather he made himself nothing'. (Phil. 2: 5–8). What they could have done they chose not to do. These were acts of sacrificial love—made for us! There can be no 'if' about that love.

BACK TO THE PROBLEM OF PAIN

Many challenge belief in an almighty, supposedly loving God who permits so much suffering in the world. How can he be just and loving without putting a stop to it? The plan Father and Son devised and accomplished met both justice (full payment of the penalty for sin) and mercy (costly compassion for wrongdoers). 'God was reconciling the world to himself in [yes, *in*] Christ' (2 Cor. 5: 19a). At great cost, God-in-Christ offers to restore the relationship with him, broken by our sinfulness.

This is the 'cross-work' that resolves the conundrum of an almighty yet loving God who still allows so much pain. Just as the resolution of a crossword puzzle hinges on the shared letter in both 'down and across' answers, so the connecting link between the descent of divine might and the extended arms of mercy is the sacrificial love of

God-in-Christ. He cares enough to pay the just price for our sins, so offering to bring us back into fellowship with him. He lovingly shares our pain and supports us in it, with hope of resurrection ahead. Committed believers have a new and living relationship with Father and Son through the Holy Spirit (Eph. 1: 17–20). It is offered freely to us because the heavy penalty was paid on our behalf at Calvary.

When the enemy tries to shake our confidence, he will quail at God's word. God's promises cannot fail, however long we may have to wait for their fulfilment. The sword of the Spirit, the word of God, is vital in protecting us from enemy attacks (Eph. 6: 12–18). We need to get to know God and his word better before the mystery of suffering is at least partially unveiled. We then find a glimpse of God's almighty, loving yet costly purposes as shown by his sharing in the life, death, resurrection and ascension of his Son. The subsequent benefits on offer are immeasurable. We gain from that shared pain.

STILL A MYSTERY BUT EASED BY GRACE

When facing such a vexed problem as human anguish we recall how, centuries ago, the Lord expressed concern about the suffering of the Hebrew slaves and acted to relieve it (Exod. 3: 7–9). His compassion has not changed. Sometimes (not always) prayers for healing are answered in this life but God's more usual response, 'Wait', is always with reason.

God sees the end from the beginning. His word assures us of a coming day when all will be made new, including our vulnerable bodies (1 Cor. 15: 42–44, 49). The hope set before us encourages us to believe and trust that God's purposes are entirely good. We cannot see them in advance but he can, and does. We have to trust that our almighty, loving God knows best, for his perspective is very different from ours.

When tempted to doubt or to fear the future, an ancient promise holds good: 'The Lord himself goes before you and will be with you; he will never leave you nor forsake you. Do not be afraid; do not be discouraged' (Deut. 31: 8).

READ, MARK, LEARN
Matthew 27: 46
John 3: 16
2 Corinthians 8: 9
Romans 5: 20–21
2 Corinthians 5: 19–21
Isaiah 53: 4
2 Corinthians 9: 15

BACKGROUND READING

Packer, J. I., *A passion for holiness*, (Cambridge: Crossway Books, 1992)

Roseveare, Helen, *Enough*, (Tain, Ross-shire: Christian Focus Publications, 2011)

Stott, John, *The cross of Christ*, (Leicester: InterVarsity Press, 20th anniversary edition, 2006)

Weinandy, Thomas G., *Does God suffer?*, (Edinburgh: T&T Clark, 2000)

CHAPTER 8

There is always a good reason for God's delays

CHILDREN ARE not the only ones who say they 'can't wait' for important occasions such as Christmas. From Genesis to Malachi in the Old Testament there are many promises of a coming Messiah, or Saviour (Gen. 3: 15 and Mal. 4: 2). Yet centuries passed before he came, and by then many had lost hope.

THE COMING OF JESUS WAS PERFECTLY TIMED
'When the set time had fully come, God sent his Son...' (Gal. 4: 4). Jesus' birth during the era of the Roman Empire was timed to coincide with a national census. His earthly father's descent from David meant that his registration must be in Bethlehem of Judah. Joseph's wife Mary was about to deliver and her miraculously conceived baby's birth in that city fulfilled prophecy (Mic. 5: 2). The Roman governor, Pilate, would eventually order his death by crucifixion, the cruellest form of execution invented by his people. The hated Roman occupation suffered by Israel thus affected

Jesus' birth and his death, being used by God to carry out his long-planned purpose for the salvation of the world.

Later, when forced to flee, early Christian believers would travel across the empire on Roman roads. These direct routes would help them to carry far and wide the good news of Jesus' death, resurrection and ascension. The apostle Paul would use some of the same roads to establish new young churches. Waiting for God's 'set time' had important implications. After such a long wait before he came, the pattern of Jesus' perfect life, agonising death, triumphant resurrection and final ascension encourages us to see that God's purposes take time to ripen, but ripen they will. He does not take short cuts. The pains of God-in-Christ finally gained the victory over sin and death, and in that we are invited to share (1 Cor. 15: 57).

HOW CAN HE BEAR IT? HE *HAS* BORNE IT!

Jesus completely understands our distress during trials if and when we feel forsaken by God. He, too, experienced dereliction on the cross as he asked his agonised question, 'Why?' In him 'we have one who has been tempted in every way, just as we are—yet he did not sin' (Heb. 4: 15). Those who have hit the bottom are able to share the pain of others in ways unknown to the pain-free. Through his Spirit he offers comfort and hope. He often speaks through God's word, or prompts others of his people to support us practically and prayerfully. He will never leave or forsake us (Heb. 13: 5).

As well as giving his life for our transgressions, Isaiah said that God's Suffering Servant 'took up our pain and bore our suffering' (Isa. 53: 4–5). Matthew applied these words to Jesus' healing of infirmities and diseases (Matt. 8: 17). Just as his death offers forgiveness of sins, so we can entrust our sicknesses to him, too. For some sufferers the valley is long whilst others experience a wonderful mini-resurrection of healing in this life. Once committed to him, we remain in God's care. Whether or not minds and bodies are totally cured in the here and now (and of course, death will come to us all) to trust the outcome to him can itself bring ease. His great and costly love for us is never ending. We pray believing that he is able to heal whilst at the same time knowing that, whatever happens, his ways are perfect and his grace unending. His purposes are always good.

JESUS KNOWS ALL ABOUT OUR TROUBLES

Our loving God foresees what good he can eventually bring out of a bitter experience because, through his death and resurrection, that is what happened to Jesus. Our tears can be lenses to bring clearer focus. Even death will lose its sting, for it will take us to join the one we have not yet seen but already respond to in love. Before returning to his Father, Jesus promised that he would come back and take his followers to be at home with him (John 14: 3). We await fulfilment of that promise, either through death or when Jesus returns (1 Thess. 4: 16–18). As we accept his pruning and keep in step with him, his Holy Spirit will continue to make us fruitful (Gal. 5: 25).

We are promised that at the end of time we will all be changed, mortality exchanged for immortality, battered old bodies for glorious new ones (1 Cor. 15: 51–54). This is the hope set before us in life, death and our darkest hours in between. Fulfilment will be the ultimate miraculous healing. Come what may, we are promised underlying peace with God and eternal assurance of his love. It is not what we deserve, but is all of his unmerited favour, his grace (Rom. 5: 1–2).

TO BE MADE LIKE JESUS IS WORTH WAITING FOR

It can be hard to wait, especially when enduring any kind of trial. When waiting trustfully on God, it is not that we are simply asking him to make things better but that his purposes will be fulfilled in our lives, to his glory. Paul tells us that God's amazing intention is to restore us back into his image (2 Cor. 3: 18). This was the original design (Gen. 1: 27) before the first couple marred it by their disobedience. The same glorious and sinless likeness was revealed in the earthly Jesus (Col. 1: 15). The loving intention is for us to become like Jesus!

This is not an instant transformation. In various ways, including painful experiences, the heavenly sculptor lovingly chips away at our resistance until he sees that lovely likeness emerging. It will be made complete when we finally see him as he is (1 John 3: 2). Jesus endured 'for the joy set before him', and with his help, so may we (Heb. 12: 2).

FELLOWSHIP IN SUFFERING

Part of God's present purpose is that the comfort he has given us will overflow into other lives. Personal adversity trains us to recognise hurt in others, an insight not given to everyone. Others gain from our past pain when we can point them to the God of all comfort. He 'comforts us in all our troubles, so that we can comfort those in any trouble with the comfort we ourselves receive from God' (2 Cor. 1: 3–7). Note well the 'so that'. Suffering could preoccupy, turning us in on ourselves. God's better plan is to use it to cross out our capital 'I' in response to his sacrificial love. Our arms can then stretch out to others in need, as Jesus extended his (Gal. 6: 2). The testimony emerging from past pains is something to be shared.

We have beside us someone who knows all about suffering, for he has overcome what no mere human could ever experience. He is silently planning for us in love. Let's keep trusting him! Sometimes he has a word of correction or rebuke we have been too busy to hear before being laid low, but he remains an ever-present help in all kinds of trouble.

ALL THE GRACE WE NEED

We have the assurance once given to a man who was in so much unidentified pain that three times he begged the Lord to heal him. The request was heard but not granted except for this loving assurance: 'My grace is sufficient for you, for my power is made perfect in weakness.' That man was Paul, who was so inspired by this promise that he was glad—even delighted—that his weakness and many hardships would speak to others of Christ's power.

Is God really almighty and caring? Our mighty God empowers the weak and our loving Lord Jesus shares his compassion with them. We can have confidence in his further words to Paul. 'My grace is sufficient for you' and learn to echo his response 'For when I am weak, then I am strong' (2 Cor. 12: 7–10).

AN EXAMPLE FROM THE PAST

Annie J. Flint was a popular American hymn writer. Only a few knew that she wrote from a wheelchair, enduring disabling arthritic pain over many years at a time when there was little pain relief. She had a frail younger sister but otherwise had no close family left. From this afflicted background, in the style of her day, she was able to write:

> He giveth more grace when the burdens grow greater,
> He sendeth more strength when the labours increase;
> To added affliction he addeth his mercy:
> To multiplied trials his multiplied peace.
>
> When we have exhausted our store of endurance,
> When our strength has failed ere the day is half done,
> When we reach the end of our hoarded resources,
> Our Father's full giving is only begun!

Fear not that thy need shall exceed his provision,
Our God ever longs his resources to share;
Lean hard on the arm everlasting, availing;
The Father both thee and thy load will upbear.

His love has no limit, his grace has no measure,
His power has no boundary known unto men;
For out of his infinite riches in Jesus
He giveth, and giveth, and giveth again!

Annie Johnson Flint (1866–1932)

READ, MARK, LEARN
Galatians 4: 4–5
Hebrews 11: 1–2, 39–40
Psalm 40: 1–3
Acts 27: 20, 23–25; 28: 1
Deuteronomy 31: 8
Habakkuk 2: 3
2 Corinthians 12: 9a

BACKGROUND READING

Flint, Annie Johnson, 'He giveth more grace when the burdens grow greater', available online at https://library.timelesstruths.org/music/He_Giveth_More_Grace/ (last accessed 16th February 2019)

Yancey, Paul, *What's so amazing about Grace?* (Grand Rapids, Michigan: Zondervan, 1997)

CHAPTER 9

Pain when gain is the chief aim

THE NATURALIST Henry Thoreau famously commented on 'the mass of men who live lives of quiet desperation' (*Walden*, 1854). He blamed this on their exclusive concentration on acquiring wealth and fame. Those who watch the stock market think of gain in straightforward financial terms but are warned that there may also be losses. Sometimes such losses are written large in the media but involve a more important investment than money. Making financial gain the main goal in life leads to pain, for we cannot serve both God and money. Devotion to one is sure to devalue the other; all too often the love of money wins (Matt. 6: 24). Mankind is still tempted to hanker after forbidden fruit, with spiritual poverty as the result.

A STORY OF UNBALANCED AMBITION

A certain schoolboy gained a scholarship to a most prestigious school. His parents saw this as opening up the way to an excellent education and a worthwhile career. If he gained entry to a top university and a good firm, they would be even prouder of him. As the young man entered upon gainful employment he became a dreamer of dreams and developed even more ambitious plans for himself.

Let's call this person Bob, and pick up his career as he heads up a well-known construction firm. He becomes a consultant for different projects in the City and chairman of various committees and working parties. His fame spreads overseas and he is in demand as an international adviser and speaker, so much so that his wife has left him. She took the children, saying that he was never there for them. He continues to be wined and dined by others and grows fat.

Meanwhile Bob's original business flourishes, but he becomes dissatisfied with some of the work done in earlier years. He decides to replace the model houses built by his firm several decades ago with buildings of a more contemporary architectural style. More orders should follow such a daring project and he makes plans to demolish the old buildings and install his bold innovations. Work is about to start when suddenly one night he experiences a restrictive pain in his chest, travelling down his left arm.

Bob's thoughts are in a whirl. A memory surfaces from his schooldays when he was head boy of his famous school. He had read the lesson at a service in chapel and rehearsed the reading so often that he still remembers some of the words:

'Watch out! Be on your guard against all kinds of greed; life does not consist in an abundance of possessions...You fool! This very night your life will be demanded from you' (Luke 12: 14–20).

The school chaplain had followed the reading with the story Jesus was telling about an ambitious farmer who, Bob hazily realises, was just like the man he has become. The farmer had been about to pull down his old barns and build bigger ones to hold the larger harvests he was planning for. It was just then that God had warned him that his life was about to end. As Bob lapsed into unconsciousness, the punch line of Jesus' story came back to him: 'This is how it will be with whoever stores up things for themselves but is not rich towards God' (Luke 12: 21).

Although Bob's story is imaginary, the parable may be true of some entrepreneurs today. We hope that a team of paramedics would arrive in time to save Bob's life and give opportunity to change his priorities. For the rest of us the lesson is clear. There is much more of value to be gained in life than is offered by money, property or prestige, and it may be later than we think.

RICH TOWARDS GOD?

To focus entirely on material gain will in the end bring pain. Selfish ambition aims at all the benefits of wealth and reputation without much thought of sharing them. The alternative, of being rich towards God, means that any rise in fame and fortune is humbly offered back to him for use in his service. He has entrusted us with any skills and assets we have in the first place. Making a priority of amassing treasure on earth, even idolising it, is to ignore the greatest commandment of all. We should love the Lord our God with *all* our heart, soul and mind (Matt. 22: 37–38). Love for our neighbour comes next but is likely to be neglected by someone so driven by ambition. Bob's broken family represents many who suffer this fate.

In his compelling little book *Dethroning Mammon* (2017), Justin Welby, the present Archbishop of Canterbury, writes about money that it 'draws our gaze away from things that are more worthy of our attention, but have not been given the badge of a comparable monetary value' (p. 40). In a materialistic society value is assessed by *size* (of car, house, income) or *status* (being on a desirable rung of the ladder). Wealth is calculated in strictly financial terms. Invisible assets, such as a loving family life, do not feature in the balance sheets, although of priceless value.

Paul warned Timothy that 'the love of money is a root of all kinds of evil' (1 Tim. 6: 10). Money is useful and not of itself evil but it should not become a major love object, for that will greatly distort clarity of judgment. Love for God should come first, then generosity to others as an overflow of that love (2 Cor. 9: 11–12). James suggested that the rich should stay humble (James 1: 10), that ostentation could lead to discrimination (James 2: 1–4) and that God honours those who are rich in faith though poor in the eyes of the world (James 2: 5).

GENEROSITY TO OTHERS

In a materialistic secular society such an aspiration is to speak in an unknown tongue, suggesting loss instead of profit. For a fair distribution those with plenty should be ready to help others who are hard pressed, but the state of our world indicates that there is a great gap between need and its supply. In comfortably off nations it should be possible for both gain and generosity to co-exist, but wealth is not always held on an open hand. It is often the poorest people who are prepared to share what little they have.

I recall my first visit to Albania when the country had only just opened up and people had been made aware of their great poverty compared with other nations. There had been an outpouring of aid, some of which (such as shabby clothes, stubs of pencils or well-worn erasers) had caused offence to a still proud people. In contrast, three of us were warmly invited home to meet some of the locals. Set before each of us was a small glassful of an unknown drink and a piece of crystallised fruit, both clearly held in reserve for a treat. It was only polite to partake and enjoy. Afterwards I noticed that the glasses of our hosts were surreptitiously emptied back into the bottle and the rest of the fruit returned to its box. It had been their generous and costly welcome to us and was very special.

It is not wrong to be rich and famous. God has promised to honour those who honour him (1 Sam. 2: 30). Godly people who have become wealthy often use their assets conscientiously and generously to further God's kingdom.

Others, though not necessarily Christian, found charities aiming to help people in dire straits, both at home and abroad. Motivation matters. Whereas some rich people are open-handed, others have mixed motives, hoping to capitalise on the gift later. Occasionally one of these same names appears in court proceedings, charged with fraud. The reputation of the whole enterprise then suffers along with those accused. According to a recent BBC television report, fraud now tops the list of crime in England and Wales.

'WHAT'S MINE'S MINE...'

In the western world, apart from special appeals, there has developed a primarily materialistic outlook, with less concern than there used to be for others in need. The temptation is to say, 'There are limits,' or to give lip service (only) with, 'There's plenty of need on our own doorstep', without any attempt to relieve it. Everywhere in the world there is a gap between the ungenerous rich and the deserving poor. Consciences may be nudged into action after a moving press release about famine victims or casualties of war, especially when children are affected. Yet repeatedly watching the same kind of news eventually makes death, disease and destruction all too familiar. Donations diminish as compassion fatigue sets in.

WORLDLY AMBITION CAN DAMAGE YOUR HEALTH

We are sometimes given a window into the world of the media and entertainment by actors, film stars, broadcasters and others who describe the competitive, even cut-throat, nature of their industries. They are not alone in that lifestyle. The price paid to achieve eminence of any kind can include stress, with overindulgence in drink or drugs. We occasionally hear of someone's sudden death from an accidental or deliberate overdose. Some will take warning in time and seek treatment for depression or burnout. A few consider withdrawal from the rat race altogether, tired of being trampled on in someone else's climb to the top.

An increasing number take on two or three jobs to support extended families or meet over-ambitious commitments. Countless marriages are put under strain by a partner's impossible schedule, perhaps taken on with hopes of promotion and a higher standard of living. In the process, once-precious relationships are demoted.

WHAT FOLLOWS THE SUMMIT?

When glittering careers reach their peak there can be a gradual decline in popularity. Falling stars are no longer considered for the key roles once enjoyed. Potentially clever business deals may crash, and future hopes with them. From being wealthy and sought after we sometimes hear of lonely, impoverished retirees, hoping to benefit from writing their memoirs. Past fair-weather friends are no more. It has been well said that deathbed regrets are unlikely to include having spent too little time at the office.

When so much of first importance has been neglected, the end of once gainful employment can be especially painful.

It is a reminder of Jesus' warning that to choose the popular broad way leads to destruction. His narrower way is much less popular but opens up into eternal life (Matt. 7: 13–14).

ALL THAT GLITTERS IS NOT GOLD

King Solomon was one of the richest men of his times, endowed by God with both wisdom and wealth to a degree previously unknown. A royal visitor who had travelled far to see all this for herself said that the reports reaching her had not done him justice (1 Kings 10: 1–7). Yet it turned out that this great king had a divided heart. Despite all his God-given blessings we read that 'his heart was not fully devoted to the Lord his God' (1 Kings 11: 4). He turned to (expressly forbidden) idolatry and ungodly marriages. This disobedience so angered the Lord that Solomon's great kingdom would be torn apart, but not until he died (1 Kings 11: 9–13). God preserved the house of Judah to keep old promises to Solomon's father, King David. Jesus the Christ would eventually be born into it (Matt. 1: 6, 16).

This same Solomon probably wrote much of the Bible's Book of Proverbs. Some sayings were possibly the sorrowful expression of hindsight: 'Those who trust in their riches will fall, but the righteous will thrive like a green leaf' (Prov. 11: 28). In one of his psalms his father had warned, 'though your riches increase, do not set your heart on them' (Ps. 62: 10). Sadly, Solomon had set his heart on riches and fell for the subsequent temptations. That was how he lost both respect and reputation.

Solomon has many contemporary successors, attracted like moths to the flickering flames of wealth and prestige, only to find them unfulfilling and potentially damaging. To make gain life's chief aim risks self-inflicted pain and can hurt others at the same time. We have been warned.

READ, MARK, LEARN
Matthew 6: 21, 24
Luke 12: 15–21
Matthew 7: 13–14
2 Corinthians 8: 11–12
2 Corinthians 9: 8
Psalm 62: 10b
2 Corinthians 8: 7b

BACKGROUND READING

Catherwood, Fred, *Light, salt and the world of business: Why we must stand against corruption* (Peabody, MA: Hendrickson, 2012)

James, Oliver, *Affluenza: How to be successful and stay sane* (London: Vermillion, 2007)

Sider, Ronald J., *Rich Christians in an age of hunger: Moving from affluence to generosity* (Nashville, Tennessee: Thomas Nelson, 1978)

Welby, Justin, *Dethroning mammon: Making money serve grace* (London: Bloomsbury Academic, 2017)

CHAPTER 10

Waste or worship?

THE LAST chapter outlined the results of misusing wealth. In contrast, Jesus often spoke of the proper use of money, for many a touchy and even painful subject.

A story is told in all four gospels about an expensive jar of perfume being poured out onto the head or feet of Jesus. The variations in the accounts suggest that similar incidents may have involved two different women. In Luke's version the giver had apparently lived a very shady lifestyle until the Light of the World illuminated and forgave her (Luke 7: 36–39). Jesus had graciously lifted her up from the gutter so that she overflowed with gratitude, pouring out her costly offering as she knelt at his feet. Failure repented of and lovingly forgiven gives a chance to start again. As we found in chapter 3, love poured out is never wasted.

Yet in three of the accounts, the gospels tell that wasteful was exactly what the watching disciples thought of the gift. They were thinking only of its market value as they added, 'This perfume could have been sold at a high price and the money given to the poor' (although their treasurer would probably have helped himself first) (Matt. 26: 6–13 and John 12: 6). Jesus pointed out that there would always be poor to be helped whenever they felt like it. Luke commented how Jesus had instead thought the woman's devoted and generous offering beautiful. It would always be remembered, across the world, as we are doing now.

Jesus perceived the motive behind the deed. The woman was making her sacrifice to anoint him before his approaching death and burial. Any pang she could have felt in parting with what possibly represented her life savings was forgotten in the joy of giving it to Jesus, and in his response. It was expensive perfume, so whiffs of it may have persisted during his harsh trial and horrible execution, bringing a sweet reminder of her love outpoured when he was so painfully pouring out his own.

The tears accompanying the gift suggest that in giving him her precious perfume the woman was offering her whole self. This is what her detractors had failed to recognise. Paul would describe such an offering as a living sacrifice, a true expression of worship (Rom. 12: 1), and warmly accepted by Jesus as such. The disciples who saw it simply as waste were ignoring both his worthiness to receive such homage and how much it revealed of the woman's depth of love. They saw without perceiving and judged only by material values.

There are still many such critics around today. They regard as wasteful the offering to God of time, talents and tithes—sometimes of life itself—by those who love him. Scoffers think of them as losers, oblivious to the fact that giving to our generous God can never match what he graciously gives to us in our salvation, preservation and all the blessings of this life.

THE GRACE OF GIVING

We have already looked at some of the potential problems of lives spent in accumulating wealth. Here the woman at Jesus' feet represents his humbler followers, setting an example for all who love our Lord Jesus. The Son of God himself has set out for us the truest pattern of giving. Despite being equal with God and sharing all his glorious riches in heaven he suffered the biggest cultural shock imaginable by his humble birth and simple lifestyle. This act of grace was to enrich us by exchanging our spiritual poverty for his heavenly wealth (2 Cor. 8: 9 and Phil. 4: 19). He 'made himself nothing', living to serve others before enduring the horrors of the cross. Afterwards he rose again to return home to his Father (Phil. 2: 3–11). His Holy Spirit offers to produce in his followers the same sacrificial love as his.

Paul urges upon us 'the grace of giving' (2 Cor. 8: 7) whereby those blessed with plenty will supply the needs of others who have less (2 Cor. 8: 14). God loves a cheerful, not a grudging, giver (2 Cor. 9: 5, 7). These are the standards expected of those instructed and indwelt by the mind of Christ, standards set by his loving generosity. Before sharing his gifts with others, we need first to have given ourselves to the Lord (2 Cor. 8: 5). Response to the self-giving love of Jesus will inspire the natural overflow of our grateful hearts. One of the gifts of the Holy Spirit is for us to contribute 'generously' to the needs of others (Rom. 12: 6–8).

PRACTICALITIES

In this context, 2 Corinthians chapters 8 and 9 are worth reading straight through. They are full of wise advice about the grace of giving. In case someone should make an over-enthusiastic response, Paul makes a very practical point. We should not bite off more than we can chew and over-commit ourselves beyond our true ability, perhaps with an over-ambitious donation. He warns that gifts are acceptable according to what one has, not according to what one does not have (2 Cor. 8: 12). His emphasis was on the willingness to share what we have.

Good stewardship of the resources God has given us means that we plan our giving prayerfully, remembering that, however it came to us, he is the source of all that we have. We must use it wisely. A familiar prayer reminds us that everything comes from God, and we give him only what comes from his hand (1 Chron. 29: 14). Jesus did not dispute the practice of giving a tenth of one's income, though richer people could give more. He warned not to be boastful about such gifts and, when distributing them, to be motivated by justice and the love of God (Luke 11: 42).

Of course, essentials such as food, clothing, housing, and for some taxation, all cost money. Children bring expenses with them, balanced by the great asset of their contribution to family love.

COUNTING THE COST

A rich young man, earnestly wanting to obey God, still found this teaching too hard. Jesus had told him to sell his possessions and give the proceeds to the poor, but he turned sorrowfully away. The cost was too high (Matt. 19: 16–22). In contrast, an old missionary, very conscious of the call to share, was found to be living in a desperate half-starved condition. He had been so overwhelmed by the needs of the people around him that he was trying to meet them all by himself, an impossible task. The willingness and the love were there but not a balanced assessment of what he could properly afford. The many appeals sent out by missionary societies look for other supporters to avoid this kind of deprivation, both in their workers and those they work amongst. Like the old missionary, we cannot rise to all the challenges coming our way but should be ready and willing to share with those specially laid on our hearts. Giving of our means may at first seem costly but to give our whole lives to God's service is to find how trustworthy he is and how faithful his loving-kindness.

God richly provides us with everything for our enjoyment (1 Tim. 6: 17–19). A young South African wanted to take a group of schoolboys to a Christian holiday camp but was short of the full fees. At the last minute a gift arrived from

England, sent by someone quite unaware of any special need. Even more remarkably, weeks before the deficit was realised the sum sent had not only used up the modest reserve of rands at the donor's Post Office but it precisely met the sum that would be required. Our God looks ahead and supplies need, not greed. As C. S. Lewis commented in his book *The four loves:* 'A secret master of ceremonies has been at work' (1963, p. 83).

NOT ALL COSTS ARE CASH COSTS

When the anticipated cost cannot be relieved by cash, God is still there to help. Faith in him means that some will go through stormy waters yet feel his presence nearer than in their calmer days. He has promised, 'Do not fear, for I have redeemed you...When you pass through the waters I will be with you; and when you pass through the rivers they will not sweep over you. When you walk through the fire, you will not be burned...since you are precious and honoured in my sight, and because I love you' (Isa. 43: 1–4).

This was the experience of Daniel's three friends. They were thrown into a burning fiery furnace for their refusal to worship the king's golden idol, but onlookers saw a fourth figure with them, walking in the flames. They all escaped unscathed, to the glory of God (Dan. 3: 1–30). Examples of absolute faith in God, regardless of outcome, encourage others facing a life-threatening crisis to trust to his abiding, supportive presence. He has promised never to leave or forsake us (Heb. 13: 5).

Some may argue, 'That's all very well, but there are still believers who drown, or are burned to death'. The tsunami of 2004 was not the only major flood to overwhelm all kinds of people. Fanatics frequently burn down the homes or churches of those with whom they disagree, sometimes with the families or worshippers still inside. Does that mean that God's promises have been broken? Never! He said, 'Fear not for I am with you', knowing full well that for some the danger will end in death. Whatever happens to the body, the essential 'you' will not be destroyed but taken to be in his even closer presence. In life, in danger and in death we can trust him to stay alongside.

IS SUFFERING A COMPLETE WASTE?

Many Indian Christians are among those overseas who are experiencing great suffering rather than denying their love for the Lord Jesus. Among them are two sisters who heard on the radio about his sacrificial love. Their responsive love for him was soon to be tested by religious extremists. The girls' newfound faith was declared a waste and their persecutors savagely, but vainly, tried to beat it out of them. Both women are now in hiding, rescued and supported by members of a Christian organisation. Like the early disciples in similar circumstances, they were able to rejoice 'because they had been counted worthy of suffering disgrace for the Name' (Acts 5: 40–41). Dishonoured in the eyes of the world but grateful to be supported by worldwide prayer, they knew the blessing of godly joy, gained from their suffering.

A CROSS-SHAPED PATTERN OF LIFE
HAS RESURRECTION TO FOLLOW

A persecuted Christian leader in a troubled country refused to flee as others were doing but wrote, 'I lost my village, my church, and now I am losing many church members who are emigrating abroad. But I see things with the light of God. When Jesus died, everyone thought it was the end of the Church. But three days later Jesus rose from the dead and now we know that his death was the beginning of the Church. When Stephen was stoned, it seemed to be the end of the Church but instead it spread Christianity.' He believed that the pains that he and others were enduring could well be labour pains, preparing to deliver new spiritual life into their beloved homeland. After the pattern of Jesus' cross and resurrection, suffering can be followed by newness of life in the lives of others as well as for the sufferer.

This is a call to a cross-shaped way of life. The vertical of our own cross is like a capital 'I' with a line going through it as we learn to love, honour and obey God's commands above self-will. What may at first have been seen as merely dutiful obedience (to be struggled with or ignored) gradually becomes the best way to live because inspired by his love. He is no taskmaster and longs for our love in return. Being human, we frequently fall short but he is ever ready to forgive and restore. His cross-bar stretched out Jesus' arms to embrace others with selfless love, forgiveness and compassion. He extends all of this to us as we seek, with his enabling, to follow his example with ours. This whole process can be painfully costly. Some may be called to forego high ambition, wealth or public acclaim to pursue a much humbler position. Whatever our particular 'cross' we will slowly become aware of enjoying deeper knowledge of and fellowship with our self-giving Lord Jesus. In his time, the Holy Spirit will move in to bring about a wonderful resurrection with newness of life, sometimes only recognised with hindsight. The painful experience eventually bears fruit in our lives that is likely also to bring blessing to others.

John Stott's father had an ambitious career in mind for his son and at first saw it as a waste of potential when John opted for theological training instead. Yet the ministry of John Stott, by spoken and written word, has had a profound influence on the understanding and practice of biblical Christianity all over the world. His long life was spent after the self-denying pattern set by our Lord Jesus, yet his face beamed with the peace and joy of his resurrected Lord.

LOVE IS WONDERFULLY COST-EFFECTIVE

Are those critics right who think that we are wasting our time in the service of God? We may be nothing special in the world's eyes, working at a very humble job or, if better paid, failing to keep up with the Joneses even when we could. The Joneses do not know (and we will not tell them) that by choosing to drive a modest old car we have enabled a Christian worker elsewhere to buy a reliable motorbike. On it he takes the good news of Jesus to an otherwise unreached community and sends back his love and thankfulness, no doubt joyfully noted in heaven as well as on earth.

Responding generously to any kind of need may involve doing without things that others consider essential in order to free up time, money or energy. To live simply that others may simply live is in theory a telling slogan; in practice it tests our willingness for a sacrificial lifestyle. In the light of the price paid by Jesus on our behalf, any cutting back entailed will be more thank-offering than sacrifice. It can later be heart-warming to learn how much one small contribution has helped someone else to 'simply live'.

The apostle Paul said, 'Do not conform to the pattern of this world, but be transformed by the renewing of your mind' (Rom. 12: 2). Such a transformation changes a sacrificial gift into spiritual harvest and any slight pain into abundant gain, for us and for others. We learn to trust when we cannot see, for 'God is greater than our hearts, and he knows everything' (1 John 3: 20). His knowledge includes awareness of our exact income and outgoings.

God is ever ready to teach us more about how to apply the grace of giving. It is part of the offering of our whole selves in love and gratitude to him who so loved us and gave himself up for us (Eph. 5: 2). To quote Paul again, this is our true and proper worship (Rom. 12: 1).

BACKGROUND READING

Guillebaud, Simon, *Sacrifice: Costly grace and glorious privilege* (Leyland: 10Publishing, 2013)

Lewis, C. S., *The four loves* (London: Fontana Books, 1963)

Open Doors prayer letters, PO Box 6, Witney, OX29 6WG, UK (www.opendoorsuk.org/resources/prayer/)

Roseveare, Helen, *Living holiness: A very moving and personal account of a journey toward godliness* (Minneapolis: Bethany House Publishers, 1986)

Steer, Roger, *Inside story: The life of John Stott* (Nottingham: InterVarsity Press, 2009)

Stott, John, *The grace of giving: 10 principles of Christian giving* (Oxford: International Fellowship of Evangelical Students, 2004)

CHAPTER 11

Faith on trial

An African pastor facing the death sentence in prison had his Bible confiscated and his legs chained. He wrote that, even so, 'it was the happiest time for me because I was put in the same cell with condemned persons and had opportunity to preach to all...It gave me the opportunity to share about heaven and about Christ.' When the authorities realised what was happening they kept moving him to other cells and eventually he met nearly all the condemned prisoners there were there. Five of them put their faith in Christ before being executed. The flood of letters coming to the pastor from overseas so impressed the authorities that they released him! During his incarceration the assurance of so much international prayer had greatly strengthened him in his ordeal and outreach.

In many parts of the world there are millions of people who are suffering persecution for their faith. Thousands of them have proved themselves ready to follow their Lord Jesus Christ to the death, even for some death on a cross.

Human venom and cruelty can be unimaginable. As early as 197 AD, the Christian writer Tertullian observed that, 'The blood of the martyrs is the seed of the Church'. New life followed their death then, and still does. Some of the reports reaching us tell how the Church is growing faster than ever before as a result of such witness, despite terrible opposition.

OTHER TRIALS

Less well known are the quiet sufferings experienced in a variety of places by workers who refuse to act against their consciences. Common overseas, this is so far happening to a lesser degree in a Western setting, although for daring to bring their Christian witness into the British workplace several medical staff members have been suspended by unsympathetic authorities. A Christian baker was in trouble for refusing to decorate a cake in a way that conformed to society's sexual norms but was contrary to his own. As the secular culture expands and threatens to dominate, so we may expect such court actions to increase. Those at risk should be praying to become so established in the love of Christ that they will be enabled to stand firm by the power of God to the glory of God (Eph. 3: 14–21). In this we can be inspired by the faithfulness of suffering believers overseas.

Helen Roseveare was an English missionary doctor in the Belgian Congo during the country's transition to independence in 1960. She had worked to the point of exhaustion to build and establish a hospital before most of it was demolished by rebel soldiers. They also held her hostage, brutally abused her in every way and threatened her with execution. She was spared by the intervention of grateful villagers whose only doctor she was.

Later she bravely returned to the same part of Africa to face more troubles and trials but wrote of her Lord, 'Participation in his suffering is necessary to each one if we are to fulfil his will in this world.' For us to know God's all-sufficiency, he must be given first place in our lives. Even when our present experience is daunting or dangerous we can rejoice that he is working out his purposes. Helen had reached these conclusions the hard way, slowly learning to cross out her capital 'I' by inviting Jesus to be complete Lord over her body, mind and spirit. Like the early apostles and many others since, she counted it a privilege to suffer with, and for, him (Acts 5: 41). After one particularly painful experience she had felt so identified with Christ's suffering that she wrote, 'Joy had come for tears. Privilege had replaced all sense of loss.' This is the outcome of reciprocal love. Knowing how greatly he has loved us is to be ready to love him greatly in return, whatever his constant care allows. To read Helen's books is to witness the growth of a soul into the likeness of Jesus.

FALSE ACCUSATION

Most of us read about and pray for these brave people without meeting any of them. Some years ago, I read in a national newspaper about Caleb, a British Christian who had set up a home for abandoned children in an Eastern European city. As the numbers grew he became too busy to check the past records of staff and supervise them properly, though he was innocent of anything worse than that. However, the consequences were disastrous. A number of members of staff sexually abused some of the youngsters, one of whom fled to tell a responsible adult. The police were notified and the guilty parties arrested, Caleb along with the rest. He was unjustly sentenced to 20 years in prison. Here was a Christian brother in trouble, and I felt prompted to write to him.

As happens in the Christian family, a good friend of mine is a legal counsellor in the same city and had met Caleb in connection with some of the children in his care. A significant number of them had been abandoned and picked up from the streets, with no record either of their names, ages or where their parents lived. All this information was required by the authorities before Caleb's home could be registered. It was frustrating to be told that he was running an illegal children's home when lack of registration was due to the required information being inaccessible. Without his care most of the rescued street children would have suffered all kinds of threats to well-being. Some may even have died.

Statements by some of the children went against him. They had been persuaded (sometimes forcibly) to agree with serious allegations of abuse by Caleb. Still young enough to believe what adults told them, they had accepted the irrational promise that by repeating the false assertions fed to them they would ensure Caleb's release. Too late they discovered the sad consequences when the home was closed and their dear 'Dad' imprisoned.

A PERSONAL ENCOUNTER

In 2010 two of us went to stay with my counsellor friend in her homeland and she arranged for us to visit Caleb in prison. By then he was several years into his sentence. We were immediately impressed by his godly manner and conversation, gaining the strong impression that a dreadful mistake had been made. Since then five appeals have failed, including one to the European Court of Human Rights, and as I write he remains a prisoner. In a recent letter he speaks of being able to forgive and serve with love those who have taken away his freedom. His sympathetic warders are impressed by Caleb's quiet cooperation in the daily toil of sweeping the dirty prison yard. This counts as a privilege because other prisoners are not allowed outside. As time takes its physical toll, much prayer is made on his behalf by supporters worldwide, but God still says 'Wait'.

It is possible that if he had paid a bribe to the court Caleb would already have been freed. For him that would be against the teaching of Scripture (Deut. 16: 19) and therefore of his conscience. When he is finally released he wants it to be with the false charges cleared from his record, to the glory of God. Meanwhile he shares his cell with a series of others, few of them easy companions, and a loud television. Times for quiet communion with God and meditation on his word are rare and precious. It is a cheer to have occasional fellowship with visitors, such as the two boys once persuaded to give false witness against him. They are now Christian young men, ready to put the record straight, but, so far, the court refuses them a hearing.

Those who can freely visit friends, attend church, or otherwise share in fellowship find it hard to imagine what it must be like to endure such a wilderness experience, year after year. What a foretaste of heaven it must be to have a brief taste of Christian companionship. Caleb's chief hope is in God, whose timing is perfect and whose purposes are always good.

GOD INTENDED IT FOR GOOD

When I pray for Caleb I often remember the story of Joseph, another who was falsely accused and endured a long prison sentence. Over many painful years he was changed from a cocky teenager to the tried and tested man who became Egypt's Prime Minister. As he looked back, his verdict on the whole harrowing experience was summed up in that simple yet profound sentence: 'God intended it for good' (Gen. 50: 20). Moses, too, spent forty years in the wilderness before, at 80 years of age, he was ready to hear and obey God's call on the rest of his life (Acts 7: 23, 30, 36).

Just as God opened up their future ways for Joseph and Moses when they had learned necessary personal lessons, so Caleb is confident that his Lord will, in his own good time, do the same for him. Letters and messages from across the world have been such an encouragement to him when feeling low.

To send assurances of our prayers is a simple act of love. The benefits to a recipient far outweigh any slight cost to the sender.

A CHANGED OUTLOOK

Caleb's supporters receive his news through an intermediary and it is clear from these bulletins that he has slowly reached a new place of surrender to the will of God. One message reported, 'If these years have taught me anything it's that my life is his and he can be totally trusted with it. I can be at total peace, even here, if instead of struggling for justice and deliverance I obey his call to love the Lord my God with all my heart, all my soul and all my strength (Deut. 6: 5) and leave my future in His hands.' He now cringes to look back on times past when he considered himself to be a mature Christian, led by God and working for him. 'It has taken these years of pain and suffering to humble me and make me realise that knowing God is far more important than anything I could do for him…and only that which is born of intimacy with him has any value to his kingdom…' Since he wrote that, he has had further severe tests of faith, needing even more prayer support, though he says that he can seriously thank God for what he has allowed to happen, for through it he knows a deeper spiritual life than would have been his out in the world.

A PROCESS OF REFINEMENT

Long ago, the famously patient Job said, 'He knows the way that I take; when he has tested me, I shall come forth as gold' (Job 23: 10). Gold-containing ore must pass through extreme heat to reveal and then lose its impurities. The final test of purity will be for the molten gold to reflect the goldsmith's face. Job, Joseph, Moses and now Helen, Caleb, and many others, have felt intense heat only to realise later that God had used the fiery trial to get rid of their dross. His goal was for them to emerge with faces reflecting the likeness of Jesus (2 Cor. 3: 18). Throughout their various ordeals he kept his promise to stay alongside (Isa. 43: 1b–3a, 5).

As I told Caleb's story to a friend, her immediate and natural reaction was, 'I think I'd have paid the bribe.' That would only have added more dross in need of refinement. Caleb and his Lord are going for pure gold.

SEEING THE END FROM THE BEGINNING

Whatever pains our Creator may allow, his purposes continue to be creative. He intends not to harm but to prosper us and give us hope for the future (Jer. 29: 11). One day, those who have patiently committed their suffering to him may finally be able to say with Caleb, 'I have learned that what he wants of me is my vital union with him daily; only then can he use me to fulfil the call he's created me for.' Whether or not that call brings Caleb out of prison, he is learning to trust his Lord completely until one future day he enters his visible presence.

When that day dawns for all God's faithful people they will consider their past sufferings to have been worthwhile. Paul endured floggings, imprisonments and still more pain and hardship for his Lord's sake, yet his conclusions still encourage others: 'Therefore we do not lose heart. Though outwardly we are wasting away, yet inwardly we are being renewed day by day. For our light and momentary troubles are achieving for us an eternal glory that far outweighs them all. So we fix our eyes not on what is seen, but on what is unseen, since what is seen is temporary, but what is unseen is eternal.' (2 Cor. 4: 16–18)

Faithfulness is tried, tested and proved in many different ways, but the same welcome awaits each one of the faithful. The King of glory will greet them from his throne, saying: 'Come, you who are blessed by my Father; take your inheritance, the kingdom prepared for you since the creation of the world' (Matt. 25: 31–40).

From being reviled and despised on earth they will reign with him for evermore in the glorious kingdom of heaven.

READ, MARK, LEARN

Job 23: 10
2 Corinthians 3: 18
Jeremiah 29: 11
2 Corinthians 4: 16–18
Genesis 50: 20

BACKGROUND READING

Carey, George and Andrew Carey, *We don't do God: The marginalization of public faith* (Oxford: Monarch Books, 2012)

Kendall, R. T., *God meant it for good: A fresh look at the life of Joseph* (Milton Keynes: Authentic Media Ltd, 2006)

Lloyd-Jones, Martyn, *Faith on trial: Psalm 73* (Tain, Ross-shire: Christian Focus Publications, 1965, republished 2011)

Open Doors prayer letters, PO Box 6, Witney, OX29 6WG, UK (www.opendoorsuk.org/resources/prayer/)

Roseveare, Helen, *Living sacrifice: Willing to be whittled as an arrow* (Tain, Ross-shire: Christian Focus Publications, 2007)

CHAPTER 12

From not loved to beloved

IT IS the custom among some Ugandan tribes, and possibly elsewhere, to name new babies after events that happened at the time of their birth. For example, 'Child of thunder' was born in a storm. Parents may even change their own names, as when they become 'Mother (or Father) of twins'. The twins themselves would be given the names commonly given to boys or girls in that kinship, so to meet one would automatically lead to enquiry about the other.

One of the saddest names I know of is in the book of Hosea. As a symbol of God's displeasure with Israel the prophet was instructed to name his little daughter 'Lo-Ruhamah', meaning 'Not loved' (Hosea 1: 6). Imagine going to school with a name like that! In today's world there are thousands of unloved children, abandoned on the streets, admitted to institutions or lost in a crowded refugee camp. Some travel unaccompanied across turbulent seas in overloaded rubber boats, hoping to find sanctuary. Each is made in the image of God, so is not to be looked down on.

Jesus said that they have angels in heaven and implied that these celestial beings seek guidance from the Father of the fatherless how best to care for such little ones (Matt. 18: 10).

UNSEEN CARERS

An old lady once wrote to tell me how as a child she had been trapped in a tunnel by a fall of sand. As she waited for her brother to run for help she was conscious of a white robed figure sitting with her, keeping her calm and comforted. The memory was still vivid over seventy years later.

I recall visiting a Romanian hospital ward full of children reputed to have been HIV positive at birth. As a result, though by then three years old, their whole lives had mistakenly been spent isolated from other children. There was very little stimulation and their dull sad faces told how unloved they were, moving one visitor to tears. With us was Patricia St John, the famous missionary author of Christian storybooks for children. She quietly said something that she sometimes wrote about, 'Don't forget, they each have an angel'. Not obvious to us then, perhaps, but the response of their heavenly Father was in time going to bring much more enlightened care to those and other deprived children, through his more visible messengers.

HELP!

In the early 1990s many TV viewers were shocked to see what had been going on in some Eastern European countries, especially in institutions housing thousands of children and mentally impaired adults. The care on offer was not worthy of that name. In societies where the very existence of God was denied there was no concept of honouring his image in those poor young people. Presumably their guardians had families at home who were, it is hoped, loved but it was hard to see any evidence of love in most of those desolate institutions. Occasional exceptions were the friendships to be observed between the residents themselves, depending on their mobility.

Institutionalised infants lay immobile in white cots with white sides that blocked out sight of all but a white ceiling or the occasional white-clad attendant. Any donated toys were locked safely away and the only method of stimulation known to such children was to rub the back of the head across the bed, producing flat bald patches. Those who managed to pull themselves to their feet would rock to and fro holding on to the battered cot-side, the constant creaking audible from outside the room. If an overseas visitor offered a sweetie, the child would not know what to do with it. Eyes without loving interaction became blank and staring, avoiding friendly overtures. In the 19th century the famous children's champion, Dr Barnardo, compared such deprived faces to 'little lamps with the light gone out'.

On a ward in one of these dilapidated places half the children were expected to die within twelve months. A few of us were visiting to represent Global Care,* a small British

---

* Global Care, Global Care House, 2, Dugdale Street, Coventry, CV6 1PB, UK (www.globalcare.org).

charity. It was the stuff of nightmares. We had gone there hoping to offer material, emotional and spiritual help in the name of Christ, who had been denied in that land for so long. The need was greater than we had imagined.

TO THE RESCUE

In an older children's ward in one such dreadful place it was noteworthy that a bedridden girl had asked a seven-year-old to come and talk to her. In such a bleak environment this suggested a flicker of hope, especially as the one invited for a chat had a face so badly burnt that her scarred eyelids had turned inside out and she looked dreadful. Bad burns on one of her hands had contracted so that she could not use separate fingers. The damage was said to be secondary to an old scald but the true story has never been clarified. Subsequent infections had totally blinded the child but despite her appearance she was obviously bright and chatty, worthy of being befriended.

This particular institution was known locally as 'The House of the Foolish'. There was no formal education on offer and this intelligent child was clearly in the wrong place. Her own mother was dead and her stepmother, appalled by her appearance, had persuaded the child's father to send her away. It was an unforgettable encounter, later provoking one of Global Care's supporters to comment, 'If you can't forget her perhaps God wants you to do something about her.' Wise words!

The charity used the name 'Lucy' for the little girl and set up an appeal on her behalf. The response was magnificent.

'The Lucy Fund' eventually covered the expense of her two separate visits to the UK for surgery as well as some upgrading of the desolate place she had come from. Surgery was funded from a charitable trust and performed by a generous plastic surgeon (since retired), making a big difference to her appearance and the use of the burnt hand. Although still completely blind she could now learn Braille. On her first visit, a teenager from her own country came as caregiver and interpreter. On their return, and a farewell visit to her so-called 'foolish' friends, Lucy was admitted to a better orphanage. Studies at the national School for the Blind followed, and finally she obtained a degree in her own language at the local university.

Early in the story Lucy was taken to the warm heart of her teenage companion's mother. This lovely Christian lady became her official guardian, ably supported by her husband. More than that, she loved and guided Lucy over the many years that held special difficulties for a blind child with unsightly facial scars. In the UK it is only relatively recently that the needs of disabled people are being recognised, however inadequately. In Lucy's homeland, just emerging from years of great poverty and oppression, children like her had no respect and were often hidden away, as she had been. Out of sight was out of thought for more than their basic needs.

In contrast, her guardian worked very hard to brighten the days for Lucy and her school friends with outings, birthday picnics and fun. She shrugged off the by no means unusual snide remarks and disdainful looks as she went about on public transport, guiding her little group of excited children like a motherly shepherdess. Later she helped to steer Lucy through the difficulties of secondary school education when she was the only blind student in an unsympathetic class. It was the same at university where she either had to record lectures on tape or be criticised for the clacking of her Braille typewriter. Fellow students often left her behind when moving to a different classroom. Now and again Lucy balked at the difficulties but finally came through with her guardian's loving encouragement and a lot of prayer from overseas supporters.

To meet the demands of higher education, a great deal of equipment was found, suitable for Lucy's use. This helped her to listen to audio-books, do research and scan the internet, working very hard to gather data for her projects. Now, decades since that memorable first meeting, she goes every weekday to Broadcasting House in the national capital. She produces and presents regular radio programmes in her own language, researching topical matters and conducting interviews with local notables, bringing compliments on her excellent journalism. Not all listeners know that she is blind.

After all she has been through, Lucy still has the sense of fun and merry laugh that she had as a child. Four of us were once travelling on a bus together when the other passengers loudly and rudely began to discuss the young girl's scarred face and blind eyes. Why was that Englishwoman wasting her time on a child like that, when so many others needed care? Suddenly, across the aisle, a cheerful little voice called out to me, 'Janetta, Janetta! La dolce vita, Janetta.' This was followed by a fit of giggles about having told how sweet life could be despite the sour conversation. It is partly her buoyancy that has brought her so far.

Lucy's supporters hope and pray that in a land where disability is still so dishonoured she will begin to speak for disabled people. Who would have thought that the abandoned, sightless and unsightly small girl, rescued from such a dreadful environment, would end up as a noted national personality? Evidently God would, and did! His loving care had been with her through all the vicissitudes of her life, never to abandon her in any fresh trials that may lie ahead.

GOD PLANS THE END FROM THE BEGINNING

God had clearly masterminded that early encounter, the pivotal comment stimulating action, the discovery of a generous-hearted surgeon and the provision of an ideal escort to England with a loving substitute mother awaiting her return. On the way she has gathered friends, generously made a degree of reunion with her original family, and grown in assurance and wisdom. All this has been in the knowledge that she is loved.

As a small girl on her last night in England, Lucy was heard to recite a list of names, evidently in prayer as she ended with, 'Thank you, Jesus. Thank you, Jesus. Amen.' We share in thanking the one who has brought her from such a dreadful start to where she is today. Along the way he has provided loving hands to support and steer her to her present position. Now, as a remarkably resilient and loving young woman she regularly attends a lively church and enjoys the Bible teaching. She is learning how much God has loved her throughout her tortuous journey and, whatever happens, will never let her go (Ps. 41: 1–3; Deut. 31: 6 and Heb. 13: 5). He delights to bring something good out of something bad and to turn pain into gain—and he has not finished with her yet!

A QUESTION:

What about all those other abandoned children, including those in our own land? Is God selective? Or do more of his people need to think how best to channel his love to them?

READ, MARK, LEARN
Matthew 9: 36
Deuteronomy 7: 7–8
Philippians 2: 1–2
Matthew 19: 14

BACKGROUND READING

Butterworth, John, *God's secret listener: The Albanian army captain who risked everything* (Oxford: Monarch Books, 2011)

Hamilton, Bill, *Albania—who cares? The exclusive inside story* (Grantham: Autumn House, 1992)

St John, Patricia, *Patricia St. John tells her own story* (Carlisle: OM Publishing, 1995)

Wagner Gillian, *Barnardo* (London: Weidenfeld & Nicolson, 1979)

CHAPTER 13

From darkness to light

MANY PARTS of the world are filled with people who struggle to keep going. They may be living a hand-to-mouth existence in famine-stricken countries, or have had homes and villages destroyed by earthquake, hurricane or war. According to a recent United Nations' estimate, 24 people *a minute* are being forced to flee from their homes (UNHCR, 2015, p. 2). Many others suffer drought, never ending bouts of sickness, or disability for which there is no available cure. It is hard to imagine what utter desolation they feel when all seems so dark.

'OUR LORD WILL HELP US'

During my time in Uganda the notoriously cruel tyrant Idi Amin took over. My work permit ended and I had to say 'Goodbye' to the young people who had studied the Bible together in my home. We realised that trouble lay ahead so had been reading in 1 Peter and Psalm 73 about how they may be called to face suffering. In his troubles the psalmist had almost lost his foothold until he turned back to God and made the Sovereign Lord his refuge. Peter's own sufferings had equipped him to encourage others.

One of the schoolboys looked very thoughtful as we parted. He told me of a murdered cousin, adding, 'Our future is not bright but our Lord will help us. He wants us to stand on our own two legs and be concentrated there.' This was a vivid version of Moses' counsel when his people were trapped between two dangerous options. He had told them, 'Do not be afraid. Stand firm and you will see the deliverance the Lord will bring you today' (Exod. 14: 13–14). Thankfully, his Lord also delivered Romegious as he continued to stand firm ('concentrated') on the promises of God, his Saviour, despite all the surrounding danger. When hope is faint it will be revived by the strong words of our loving Lord, recorded in the Scriptures. Help also comes from the prayer support of others.

A LITTLE LIGHT IN THE DARK

One Sunday morning I joined a company of Albanians who were holding their service in a school building. The previous atheistic ruler, Hoxha, had destroyed all churches and mosques apart from one or two left as museum pieces. Our lecture theatre was without windows and lit only by electric lights. Rows of benches raked down from the back of the room to the central dais at floor level. The room was full of people ready and eager for spiritual nourishment.

I don't now recall the sermon, but have clear memories of a little parable acted out before us as the service ended. We had begun to extricate ourselves from the benches ready to leave when there was a power cut. This was not unusual in Albania at that time but the room was immediately plunged into total darkness, the only exit being through a door at ground level. To reach it involved negotiating the steep slope of unlit steps and, afraid of falling, most people were reluctant to move. There was no panic but some confused jostling.

Suddenly a little light appeared in the doorway below. A young boy was standing there, holding up either a small torch or a candle, and beyond him we could just see sunshine. By heading in that direction, we eventually emerged safely. It had taken a single glimmer of light to give us enough guidance but the boy had held it up high. We were led out of darkness into the bright light of day, our worries relieved. Confused people had found direction through the lad's willingness to help us. He may well have had other ideas about what to do after the service, perhaps going to find a drink or meet a friend. He possibly made some small sacrifice to help us, though in truth he was probably thrilled to have become so important!

We may sometimes jib at the cost involved in serving others, be this in terms of status, time, or cash. The small boy and his light perhaps help us to recall that the cost can be minimal for the results to be great. The child had offered hope for a safe way out of the darkness, from confusion to clarity. For many living without hope we may sometimes be able to do the same, perhaps linking needy people with helpful organisations such as the Money Advice Trust (once Credit Action) in the UK, or by supporting aid agencies overseas. Now and again we have opportunity to share a greater gleam, never to be extinguished.

THE LIGHT OF THE WORLD

Many readers will be familiar with Holman Hunt's evocative painting of someone standing outside a darkened house. The heavy, ivy-covered door had clearly been kept closed for a very long time, its only handle being inside the house. The person waiting outside evidently represents the thorn-crowned Jesus. He is knocking on the door, a lantern held high in his free hand. The earthly Jesus once called himself the 'light of the world' and the artist gave the same title to his picture. By painting such a poignant scene, he intended to portray a heart long closed to the Saviour. He patiently waits to be invited in, longing for his light to dispel the darkness.

When Jesus claimed to be the light of the world he also promised the light of life to those who opened up their lives to him and were willing to follow his leading (John 8: 12). His light would then shine through them to illuminate a world in spiritual darkness. The Light of the World gave his all as a living sacrifice to enlighten mankind. Holman Hunt had written on the back of his work, 'Forgive me Lord for keeping you waiting so long'. That is a prayer for all who live shadowed lives, especially those oppressed by painful experiences.

The Saviour longs to banish their darkness for evermore by taking his light into their lives. How will he do that?

HANDING ON THE FLAME

It could have been when Jesus' Sermon on the Mount was well under way that night fell and he pointed out to his disciples the twinkling lights of a city on the distant hillside, standing out so clearly across the darkening valley. He said that they must let their own lights shine as brightly. 'You are the light of the world', he told them (Matt. 5: 14–16). His followers were to share with other needy folk the illumination he had given them, not keeping it just for themselves.

I once flew over Johannesburg as it was getting dark. Below us blazed the lights of the city and beside me were men whose job it had been to supply them. They were gratified to look down on the bright electric or neon lights, the results of their labours. Brilliant as they were, though, the individual lights could not light any other. Only a flame can readily do that.

On a different African evening, when on vacation with my ageing father, two little candles stood on our meal table, only one of them alight. As it started to burn down my father picked it up and used the last of its flame to light the second candle. Nothing was said but I knew what message he intended to convey. The candle he held had needed to melt in order to keep the flame burning and would soon have melted away, utterly spent. His light on earth would soon be quenched but he hoped that he had kindled others, including mine. Now he looked forward to his entry into the brightness of the heavenly city, where they need neither candle nor sunshine 'for the Lord God will give them light' (Rev. 22: 5). He is not only the light of the world but the light of heaven as well. In order for his light to shine from our lives, some of us may need to be willing to unbend, to melt a little, on behalf of those needing help to find light in their darkness.

THE LIGHT OF LIFE

One of my father's customs had been to hand out Gideon Bibles and New Testaments or other little booklets quoting various related verses of Scripture, his address stamped on the cover. He was not at all choosy about the recipients and one day we were driving along in my car when we came across a motorcyclist standing beside his blazing machine. Firemen, an ambulance and a police car were already on the scene, and within minutes, so was Father! Despite my protests that this was not a good moment for him to barge in, he saw it as a golden opportunity to give the shocked cyclist what he hoped would be a timely word. Mission accomplished he quickly got back in the car and I confess that it was a rather disgruntled daughter who drove on.

Years later, when terminally ill in hospital, my father received a letter from that motorcyclist. Reminding him of the incident, the young man went on to say, 'Thank you for that little book you gave me. It changed my life.' Even in the midst of flames that could so easily have taken over, a beam from the Light of the World had been shed into his inner darkness. Rather late in the day, I was rebuked and now try to keep a few of those little books with me. Only once has a copy been refused.

SHARING FAITH NEED NOT BE COMPLICATED

We need to be sensitive to the Spirit's prompting as we pursue our daily lives. He knows that on our way we may meet someone who is ripe, even desperate, for spiritual input. Sometimes the connection begins by our asking for something (even if only to know the time or, in the UK, what weather is on the way!) Jesus selected someone very unlikely when he asked a Samaritan woman drawing water at a well to draw a drink for him, too. He seized the opportunity to draw out and meet her deeper need, something we are often slow to do. Instead he began a significant conversation, aroused her interest, and stayed longer in the area to offer more teaching to everyone there (John 4: 4–42). God brought great gain from such a common need as thirst, not only for the woman at the well but for others who still benefit from that story.

As Paul had modelled and then written to his spiritual son, Timothy, 'Preach the word; be prepared in season and out of season; correct, rebuke and encourage—with great patience and careful instruction' (2 Tim. 4: 2). Preaching need not be from a pulpit, or even use many spoken words. The undiluted word of God can give the necessary message, for it is alive and active (Heb. 4: 12). It can beam the light of hope into the darkness of despair, for everything recorded in God's word was written to teach us. Through the endurance taught in the Scriptures we find encouragement and hope (Rom. 15: 4).

LET IT SHINE

When I was working in Uganda, President Idi Amin took over and there was much civil unrest. The conversation round the dinner table frequently reverted fearfully to the prevalence of burglary and the violence meted out by those known as *kondos*. I lived alone and one night with some apprehension spotted through the window a group of strangely silent local people, gathered on my doorstep. A second look showed them to be a group of schoolboys studying under my outside light—a new application of Jesus' command to let our light shine!

Of course, Jesus was referring to the spiritual enlightenment that he gives to and through us. How important it is that we walk in that light, day by day (1 John 1: 5–7).

An old proverb says, 'It is better to light one small candle than to curse the darkness.' It is even better when we can hold up the Light of the World to guide those who have lost their way.

READ, MARK, LEARN
Isaiah 9: 2
John 1: 4–5
1 John 2: 9–10
Acts 13: 47

BACKGROUND READING

Gideons International, The (Western House, George St, Lutterworth LE17 4EE and online at www.gideons.org.uk)

Lifewords (1A The Chandlery, 50 Westminster Bridge Road, London, SE1 7QY and online at www.lifewords.global)

UNHCR, 'Global trends: Forced displacement in 2015' (report, 2015)

CHAPTER 14

Hope at wits' end corner

A YOUNG WOMAN spoke with evident emotion of how trapped she had felt as a heroin addict. To maintain the habit, she stole whatever money she could find, including her little sister's meagre pocket money. It seemed to her that the drug was the only friend she had, but under its influence she lost her job and crashed her car. It was at the subsequent court hearing that her mother angered her by reluctantly reporting the addiction. The disclosure led to an order for specialist help instead of a prison sentence. Afterwards she could say that 'what Mum did was good'. She realised how blessed she was that her loving family still stood by her. I just wished (and prayed) that she would come to know a loving heavenly Father who faithfully does the same.

Throughout the Bible we have examples of people who emerged from different kinds of suffering with changed priorities. Their stories are preserved as a permanent record, ever ready to enlighten and encourage us. From Abraham in the Old Testament (Gen. 21: 5–7) to Zacchaeus in the New (Luke 19: 5–8) we read of those whose personal encounters with God were for them the turning point in life. One of the Old Testament stories on this theme is about Elijah the prophet and a widow he once helped in a place called Zarephath (1 Kings 17: 7–24). Under God, with Elijah's help the widow would find that good eventually came from her repeatedly bad experiences. Rounding wits' end corner can lead to fresh vistas.

A HUNGRY MAN FINDS HELP FOR ANOTHER'S NEED

God had first warned Elijah of a serious drought ahead and the prophet listened carefully to the bad news. It came as a tough assignment to inform Israel's king about it. Ahab was a very wicked, idolatrous man, inclined to fierce anger, who already saw Elijah as a trouble maker (1 Kings 18: 16–17). He would react sceptically to Elijah's message but would have to think again when, just as he had been warned, there followed a total lack of rain for three and a half years with subsequent severe famine. God's message and his messenger should be heeded.

For the prophet to escape Ahab's mounting wrath, God led him into hiding, well out of the king's reach. At the start of the drought a brook supplied Elijah with water and heaven-sent ravens brought him basic food. Then the stream dried up. God again told him to move on, this time directing him to Zarephath. To outline on a map Elijah's ports of call shows how far he had to walk. By the time he reached his final destination he would be footsore, exhausted, hungry and thirsty. He probably felt like one of today's refugees, far away from his homeland and facing the unknown. Neither had he escaped the famine, for the winged providers of the food drop had now flown away.

Enter the widow. Like so many in today's developing world she was nearing the end of her food supply and ready to die, her young son with her. The record tells of Elijah's request to her for a little food and water. Despite her own desperate state, she graciously gave him a small loaf, a drink of water, and shelter. She was then amazed when, as the prophet had foretold, the oil and flour she needed for baking never ran out. She realised that Elijah was in the care of a unique miracle-working God. Unlike the lifeless idols she had been worshipping it had taken a living, loving Lord to intervene and save their lives.

Then another disaster struck. The widow's beloved son fell ill and died. Like many others suffering such a crisis, she thought she was being punished for an unspecified sin. In fact, God was working out his purposes. With a fervent prayer for the Lord's help, it is conceivable that Elijah was inspired to carry out a variant of the manoeuvre used by first aiders today* and the boy breathed freely again. We can enter

---

* The Heimlich manoeuvre is used to dislodge something blocking the main airway. It involves three sharp thrusts to the abdomen or chest. Both would be compressed by Elijah's bigger body as he lay on the child three times.

into the widowed mother's relief and gratitude as she again recognised the hand of the true God at work through Elijah. Twice death had been banished from her home. It seems that this caused the woman to put her trust in Elijah's God.

DIFFERENT KINDS OF SUFFERING

Elijah must have had to nerve himself to obey God, gain access to a hostile king and deliver the unwelcome message. The flight to Zarephath may well have worn him out and at times perhaps he thought that God was expecting too much of him. In her turn, the widow spent her failing energy in gathering sticks to light the fire for baking a last small meal. In despair already, her heart must have sunk further when Elijah asked her to make a bread roll for him. Torn between her family's needs and the rules of hospitality, she generously chose to share what she had with a stranger. Elijah probably looked in even worse shape than she felt and her heart was touched.

For so many families still, demand exceeds supply and economic hardship is a painful reality. Even in Britain, the multiplication of food banks indicates that this is so for some living here as well as for thousands overseas. One extra demand can be the last straw when already under pressure, and not everyone responds as generously as that widow.

DOES ANY OF THAT SOUND FAMILIAR?

Intense emotional strain, physical weakness, important orders to be fulfilled, smouldering doubts about the rightness of a project, or whether earlier guidance had either been misunderstood or God had not been the one to give it—Elijah could have suffered all these painful misgivings. Perhaps we, too, have known them. Undoubtedly many who inhabit the world's worst trouble spots must frequently do so. In a testing situation it can be tempting to ask, 'Has God forgotten us? Have we misheard, misinterpreted or even imagined his earlier directions? Is he concerned about us at all?'

If Elijah had earlier known some of those doubts, he now saw where God had wanted him to be and why he had led him there. The widow, who had not known the true God before, went over a switchback of emotion from despair to wonder, then from desperate grief to elation. Through it all she gradually came to realise the goodness of Elijah's God.

GOD'S TIMING IS PERFECT

It was just as Elijah had reached the gates of Zarephath that he met the widow. The few minutes it would have taken her to collect a few sticks was the exact interval when, after days of walking, the prophet arrived, saw her and called out his urgent request for a drink and a little food. Because she invited him to share her limited hospitality, he was there to help when her child fell ill and died. If their paths had not crossed when they did, their stories would have had such different endings.

It is said that human extremity is God's opportunity, and he knows the exact time to intervene and how to do it. Faith may be stretched to the limit before he does so, but

TO KNOW GOD IS TO TRUST HIM,
AND TO ENCOURAGE OTHERS TO DO SO TOO

Elijah knew his God. He could confidently tell the desperate widow that her needs would be met until the drought was over. He had sensed in his spirit that the God who had specifically led him to this place would not leave him now. He shared this confidence with the woman. We can imagine her daily suspense before finding that the exhausted supplies of flour and oil had been replenished overnight. She and her household were saved. She did not know the prayer requesting daily bread that Jesus would later teach (Luke 11: 3) but Elijah's probable version of it was heard and answered. He had encouraged her to believe the promise of the Lord his God, given first to him and shared with her. Their daily bread was supplied, baked new every morning.

When her son died, that crisis shook the widow's newfound trust until Elijah's further prayer was answered. From despair in the shadow of death she and her son were twice brought back into newness of life, making her still readier to believe in Elijah's God.

SWING HIGH, SWING LOW

As with the widow, it is not unusual for an experience of God's wonderful intervention to be followed by a time of despair. The very next chapters in Elijah's own story

(1 Kings 18–19) tell how he was used to bring about an even greater manifestation of God's power, but then ran from the scene, afraid for his life. God dealt gently with his exhausted and depressed servant before a greater revelation of his power. He then sent him back the way he had come. By then he was refreshed, reassured and ready for a new task, this time with a like-minded helper (1 Kings 19: 15).

Some of us have known such times of anti-climax followed by a new commission. I recall applying for a post in Yorkshire and was happy to be invited for interview. At the time I was working as a locum in the Shetland Isles, north of Scotland's mainland. On the day I should have flown south, all planes were grounded by fog! I missed the interview, someone else was happy to be appointed and I was accordingly disappointed. Later a much more suitable post came up in the same city and was given to me. That was not the only brick wall I have met, yet in his good time God has always opened up a way through. We slowly learn to replace the d in disappointment with H, for His appointment.

THE ANSWER TO OUR 'WHY?' CAN BE GOD'S 'WAIT'

Before reaching Zarephath, Elijah had left Israel and crossed over the border into Syria's Sidon. He was to pioneer in new territory where God first revealed his power to a single mother at the end of her tether. No-one is unworthy of his loving attention, however humble they may be. Jesus would cite this venture as marking an early outreach to the Gentiles (Luke 4: 24–26).

God had also led Elijah there and back again to teach his servant (and us) an important lesson. Whatever the difficulty and however great the challenges we face, our loving Lord is to be trusted to lead us on in ways of his choice. We sometimes need the lesson to be repeated before we learn to relax into his care when he takes us from one crisis to another. After a time of painful perplexity or hardship, perhaps a long time afterwards, we too may see that the divine purpose has been to fit us for a new sphere of influence.

The widow of Zarephath simply trusted Elijah's confidence in God. In our own times of crisis, we can receive his word directly for ourselves. As we await more light on our way, something in our daily reading sometimes acts like a heavenly signpost. 'This is the way; walk in it' (Isa. 30: 21) has been used to direct an unknown number from uncertainty to trustful obedience.

If we truly believe in our Lord's omnipotence and faithful love, can we not lean back on both these aspects of his strength, relying on him to overrule in all our troubles, vexations and hesitations? Whether in accordance with our own wishes or not, he will do as he has promised, and in all things work for the good of those who love him, and are called according to his purpose (Rom. 8: 28). As with Elijah, part of that purpose can be to bring others to love him, too. We may be used to help needy people to walk round wits' end corner and find him waiting for them there. Some may then be transformed by his grace and love to become joyful in hope, faithful in prayer and even patient in affliction (Rom. 12: 12).

As we wait for his purposes to be fulfilled despite all our difficulties, and ask for his strength to see us through, we find greatest encouragement in the example of our crucified Lord. 'Consider him who endured such opposition from sinners, so that you will not grow weary and lose heart.' (Heb. 12: 2–3)

READ, MARK, LEARN
Acts 9: 23–24
Acts 16: 22–28
Isaiah 30: 19
Isaiah 40: 31
Hebrews 12: 2–3

BACKGROUND READING

Kendall, R. T., *These are the days of Elijah: How God uses ordinary people to do extraordinary things* (Ada, Michigan: Chosen Books, 2013)

Myer, F. B., *Elijah and the secret of his power*, available at: www.baptistbiblebelievers.com (last accessed 2nd January 2019).

CHAPTER 15

Never the same again

For many people in today's world, plans can suddenly lie in ruins and lives change for evermore. It is not unusual to hear of religious fanatics bursting into a previously quiet and peaceful community, bringing violence and murder, especially to those holding other beliefs. I read in a prayer letter this very morning of a small Christian community whose church had been destroyed in this way. Instead of being able to worship together in the former dedicated building, lovingly built by their own hands, they were holding their services under a tree. Despite the sudden fear, loss and insecurity, they were holding on to their Lord in faith.

Centuries ago there was a Jewish teacher of the law who was envoy to a group of religious extremists. As a strict Pharisee, he was incensed by the spreading conviction among some hitherto loyal Jews that the Christ, their long-awaited Messiah, had come and was named Jesus. They were proclaiming that he had been betrayed, killed and then amazingly restored to life before returning to God, his Father. Later, the Holy

Spirit of Jesus had descended to energise and inspire his bereft followers. This new teaching made our zealous Pharisee so angry that he was ready to charge believers with blasphemy and condone their execution.

Jesus himself had been similarly accused before he was sentenced to crucifixion. Now it was in the power of his resurrection, mediated through his Spirit, that some of his followers were bravely facing death (Acts 7: 55–8: 1). Continuing threats did nothing to put them off preaching and teaching the good news of Jesus and his love. Thousands came to believe that they would receive eternal life by believing that the Lord Jesus Christ had died in their place. Their broken relationship with God was restored. Clearly, fanaticism is not the way to win people.

The bigoted opponent of this new movement was Saul. He stood by and approved when the first martyr, Stephen, was killed. He was so infuriated by the spread of the new faith that he gained permission from the high priest to take captive and bring back to Jerusalem any believers he could find. As the Authorised King James Version of the Bible so graphically puts it, he was 'breathing out threatening and slaughter against the disciples of the Lord' as he headed for Damascus to hunt them down. On the way he was suddenly stopped in his tracks by a blinding light from heaven and a clear voice challenging his behaviour. By persecuting the young Church in what he thought was zeal for God he was actually persecuting their risen Lord Jesus, who now addressed him (Acts 9: 1–19).

Saul was destined to become the great apostle Paul. That encounter with the resurrected Jesus on the Damascus road brought his murderous quest to a sudden halt. His life was turned completely upside down by receiving a new mission from Jesus. First, he was to enlighten his fellow Jews that this was indeed their long-awaited Messiah, Son of God. Then, when they rejected this message, he was to take the good news to the Gentiles (Acts 9: 28–29 and Acts 13: 45–48). It had taken a sudden dramatic experience to break down his ingrained habits of thought. Fresh channels were being opened up to convey the new message of loving, transforming, divine grace to those who had never heard about it before.

CONTEMPORARY CHALLENGES

Many people today have suddenly lost what had been a well established lifestyle to become fugitives with an uncertain future. Shock can bring the impetus to flee or the inertia of fear, each offering a different risk of more hazards ahead. The painful choice may lie between a boat likely to sink, or slow starvation. Few will hear a clear voice telling them what to do, as Paul did. In the panic to make a decision, some will drown, some fade away without access to aid, and some survive somehow, not knowing what will happen next. Without help or hope, how can anything good come their way?

Closer to home, many experience abrupt unemployment, loss of status, sudden bereavement, accidents and injuries, abducted children and more. Personal, professional or political agendas can be thrown into disarray in an instant. Even a planned retirement can be acutely disorientating. The way ahead is no longer as plain as it had seemed a week ago.

FAITH IN GOD IS NOT AN INSURANCE POLICY

Christians are not immune from any of these disasters and distresses, although God promises his people that he will stay alongside as they endure them (Ps. 23: 4 and Isa. 43: 1–3a, 5a). Paul spent frequent periods in prison and endured at least eight severe floggings. For most of us that would have been more than enough suffering to last a lifetime, but it was only the start of the catalogue he gave of his dangers, discomforts and near-death experiences. Most of them happened during his missionary journeys (2 Cor. 11: 21b–33). In addition, he had some unspecified recurrent affliction that troubled him, despite fervent prayer to be relieved of it. The relief he was given was the promise of sustaining grace rather than of cure (2 Cor. 12: 7–10).

PRAYER CHANGES THINGS — AND PEOPLE

In times of crisis the mind can be too disturbed to focus on more than SOS prayers. The grace of God and his strength may then be channelled through others. From survivors of different disasters overseas come grateful messages in response to practical aid and loving words from people they have never met. Such prayerful encouragement has provided real strength in times of trouble when a familiar world has been turned upside down. It can also be life-saving.

Alison ('Ali') was a friend of mine who had not been a Christian for very long. Since birth she had been paraplegic (due to *spina bifida*) and became wheelchair bound. During a holiday overseas, someone else's heartless behaviour had left her so depressed that she thought God was telling her to end it all. Her inconsiderate companion had left her stranded upstairs in their holiday apartment with a tantalising view of the swimming pool below. Beside it was a girl wearing a tee-shirt displaying the message, 'Stay alive in '85'. As New Year 1986 was imminent, in her confusion Ali interpreted this as heaven-sent permission to die once it had dawned. Home again, she had an overdose ready to take on the due date, when the phone rang.

The caller wanted to wish her a happy New Year but then heard how *un*happy she was. They were miles apart but no more than a prayer away from God's love in action. Along the earthly telephone wire and even more speedily heavenwards, the request was made that the depression would lift and the pills go back in the box. By then it was after midnight so another phone call was made from England to prayerful Christians in Australia, well into their New Year's Day celebrations but very ready to give prayer support to someone in need on the other side of the world. A promise from God's word replaced the great deceiver's message, and the corner was turned. There would be a new kind of life ahead in '86.

AUTHENTIC WORDS FROM THE LORD

Any supposed 'word from the Lord' must be in accord with what is recorded for us in the Bible. Our lives are in God's hands. He both gives and takes them away (Job 1: 21). Suicide always leaves others distressed and guilty.

Ali's story had a happier ending, great gain emerging from her pain. Christian friends rallied round in 1986, offering emotional and spiritual support as she gradually learned to commit the rest of her life to God. In so doing she found that he gave her a new zest for living and someone like-minded to share her home. Together they reached out to many others who were disadvantaged and disabled. By travelling, writing and giving media interviews they acted as voices for the voiceless, especially on pro-life issues. Ali had undertaken some of these activities before, but now the known presence and power of God made all the difference. To have a kindred spirit in this work was added strength and inspiration.

Over the years, as Ali's mobility and activities diminished, the deepening relationship with her Lord acted as spur and solace. Despite great pain, her last days were spent in the consciousness of his love. Before she died she said that the greatest gift she could offer God was her suffering, hoping that, through her testimony, others would be helped to appreciate value and purpose in it. Countless people have gained from her testimony. Ever since that critical crossroads, prayers have been abundantly answered for her, right through to the end.

IT TAKES TIME TO SEE HOW GREAT BLESSING CAN FOLLOW GREAT DISTRESS

An elderly lady once said to me, 'At one time in my life I seemed to have blow after blow'. She did not spell out the nature of the blows, but the remark was prompted by sympathy for someone else currently undergoing a hammering. A fellow feeling for other sufferers is one of the positive consequences of personal pain, though it should be expressed sensitively. 'I know how you feel', can never be completely true. Safer ways to express a fellow feeling could be a bunch of flowers, a hug or an offer to pray.

At what was probably the lowest ebb of my life I heard from someone who had suffered overseas with the loss of a stillborn and deformed baby, her only child. Her husband had been under orders to attend a distant court hearing, meaning that, apart from her Lord's presence, she faced the tragedy—and funeral—alone. I was ignorant of all this when I confided my woes to her but later I would recognise the mature insight behind her understanding comment, 'God has entrusted you with this'. At the time I thought he had made a big mistake! Much later I realised that he had indeed had purposes to be achieved through that troubled time. Perhaps one of them has been the writing of this book.

Specific benefits may eventually follow personal pain. It is said that more blind than sighted people are spiritually aware—a gift well worth having, but often appreciated only gradually. At our regional cathedral I sometimes saw a blind man, John Hull. He was a university lecturer in theology who had slowly lost his sight. A film has been released, based on his audio journals, portraying the sequence of his reactions as vision faded. From understandable dismay and depression over the loss, even of visual memory, he slowly came to regard his disability as a gift from God. He is quoted as saying. 'It was not a gift I had wanted, but it was nevertheless a gift'. Slowly he came to realise more clearly his place within the loving oversight of God. One reporter aptly described the film as being about 'losing sight but gaining vision'.

It can be a struggle for some to accept that God sees a personal calamity coming but does not intervene, even though he did not cause it. Terrorism strikes, not God. A driver is responsible for cutting alcoholic intake before speeding to the spot where the car will hit a small relative of ours. I can't think that these tragedies are planned by God but he foresees, allows and can creatively work through them. Those who turn to him for comfort have so often found him to be lovingly sustaining them in ways unknown before. Others may not consciously do so but sometimes still speak gratefully of 'someone' having helped them through.

When the agony is raw there will be little comfort in a well-intentioned comment that God can bring great good from it, though people of faith learn by experience to trust this truth even in the dark. Sometimes people channel their immediate grief into helping an appropriate good cause 'to try and stop someone else going through what we've suffered.' Even that is a creative response, inspired by our great Creator.

HAVE WE TRIALS AND TEMPTATIONS?

In the small frustrations of everyday life, it can be hard to offer each minor irritation to God, trusting him to use these unwanted stresses for good. Whether they are great or small we can slowly learn to respond with patience in such negative experiences. This will enhance his glory and may also advance our own spiritual growth. Potters pummel and mould the clay because their inner eyes tell them what lovely thing can be made from it. Just so, our heavenly Father sees what he could develop by softening our resistance to his creative hands. They are able to bring good out of some of life's less than good moments. If we learn to submit even our small annoyances into those loving hands we will be readier to do so should we later have to face much greater trials.

Yet we remain human and vulnerable!—and God's intentions will only be completely fulfilled when at the end of our earthly lives we go to meet him and are made like him. This is the lovely image that he desires to reveal in all lives given to him. 'We know that when Christ appears we shall be like him, for we shall see him as he is' (1 John 3: 2). Only then will life be joyfully and for evermore free of catastrophe, filled with praise to the one who has at last brought us safely into the peaceful haven of his presence, never to be the same again.

 **READ, MARK, LEARN**
John 10: 10
Jeremiah 18: 1–4
Philippians 4: 12–13
Revelation 21: 1, 4
2 Corinthians 3: 18

BACKGROUND READING

Pollock, John, *Paul the apostle* (Eastbourne: Kingsway Publications, 1969)

Harte, Colin, *Suffering for what we value: The legacy of Alison Davis* (London: No less human, 2014); see also the video lecture by the same title at www.spuc.org.uk/news/videos/national-conference-2014/2014/september/dr-colin-harte (last accessed 15th February 2019)

Middleton, Pete and James Spinney (writer–directors), *Notes on blindness*, London: Artificial Eye (2016)

Wright, Tom, *Paul: A biography* (London: SPCK, 2018)

CHAPTER 16

The productivity of pressure

THE TROOPING of the Colour is an annual British pageant, watched by thousands in person and on television. Two hundred and fifty years ago, 'the colour', or regimental flag, rallied embattled troops for combat. Now the ceremony is performed by the Household Guards on the reigning monarch's official birthday, a different regiment presenting its flag each year. On the surface it looks almost effortless. Yet there are 113 orders of command to be remembered and obeyed by over a thousand army personnel. Cavalry and foot soldiers respond in perfect synchrony, looking splendid in their red and gold uniforms with traditional black bearskins on their heads. To the music of brass bands, they carry out amazing marches and manoeuvres, on foot and on horseback. Currently Elizabeth the Second is on the throne and as each company marches past, heads turn smartly towards her and she graciously acknowledges them in turn.

What hard work goes into it all, from the diligent polishing of the shiny boots (and hooves) to remembering each step and sequence of the complicated drill. There must be moments of exhaustion and possibly mounting anxiety over the sheer grind of the discipline involved. It all has to go on around regular military duties yet comes together as a worthy offering to the monarch. There must be immense pressure to be ready for the great day, but the final focus is not on the stressful preparation. Instead faces glow with the pride of another successful presentation, fit for a queen.

SOMETHING MORE GOING ON

Much tougher discipline is needed to prepare the armed forces to defend Queen and country. Behind the scenes, harsher parade grounds and more demanding field exercises train them to reach top form unaccompanied by cheers from an admiring crowd. When duty or danger calls they must immediately obey orders, whatever hazards and hardships may follow.

In a letter to his 'dear son' Timothy, Paul uses a similar model for good soldiers of Jesus Christ (2 Tim. 2: 3–4). If we have once trusted him as Lord of *all* then he is able to make even the most taxing routines work for our good as we offer them to him as a gift of love (Rom. 8: 28). His Spirit can trim away any reluctance to obey, encouraging instead the growth of forbearance and self-control (Gal. 5: 22). Like the Queen's Household Guards, we need to keep practising disciplined cooperation with our leader before the Spirit of Jesus will achieve God's desire in us, 'to be conformed to the image of his Son' (Rom. 8: 29). This sacrificial offering of self to him is what Paul defines as a true and proper act of worship (Rom. 12: 1).

SERVICE, WORSHIP AND SACRIFICE

The same Greek word indicates both worship and service. As with many words that have two meanings, it is easy to focus on one and neglect the other. Too often, 'the worship' has come to refer primarily to exuberant singing, usually in the company of others. It is a way of speaking to God and to each other, usually referred to in Scripture as praise, or making music to the Lord (Ps. 27: 6; Eph. 5: 19 and Heb. 13: 15). Biblical references to worship involve bowing the knee or lying low before him (Matt. 28: 9). The only scriptural mention I find to singing that accompanies worship is in heaven! (Rev. 15: 2–4) Enthusiasm for having a good sing must never drown out the sober call to offer up to God our whole selves—body, mind and spirit. This is the service of worship that honours him most, following as it does the example of our Lord Jesus Christ.

Under pressure, making music may be more an act of will than a spontaneous outpouring. A continually yielded will becomes a daily offering to him who loved us and gave himself up for us. Unwelcome events are never outside our Father's control. We slowly learn to offer them up to him, to be used for his loving purposes. Our usual idea of sacrifice can be of something grand and ambitious, yet it may be the self-denying offering of life's common pains and pressures that our Lord will use most creatively to his glory.

Our Lord Jesus humbled himself to take on the very nature of a servant before God exalted him to the highest place, and to become like him means taking on that same attitude of humility (Phil. 2: 5–8). If only we could remember, the trying experiences of daily life become opportunities for humble acceptance instead of letting ourselves get rattled. Sometimes hindsight will make clear how God has been working for good through the difficulties.

PERCEIVING WHAT LIES BELOW THE SURFACE

In nature we find many examples of the productivity of pressure. Opals owe their lovely iridescence to trapped air or water in silica, compressed far below the earth's crust; diamonds are the result of intense heat and pressure affecting carbon so deep in the earth that it took an erupting internal volcano to throw it up within reach of the surface. Much humbler but still prized, coal is made from the dead wood of ancient forests subjected to downward pressure. In all these transformations it has taken a very long time before the end products have formed. To sentient creatures, being subjected to such force for so long would be unbearably painful. Yet in time our various human pains and pressures can also produce wealth, of a different kind.

In 1966 there was a terrible disaster in the Welsh mining village of Aberfan. A huge mound of colliery debris slithered down onto a primary school, killing 116 children with 28 adults and plunging the whole community into deep mourning. When interviewed fifty years later, one of the survivors spoke movingly of how their deep grief had progressed over time. A group of women of different ages had regularly met together during that half century, all personally affected by the tragedy. First drawn together by loss, their friendships have become increasingly valuable. 'At first,' their spokeswoman said, 'the pressure of the pain was black, like coal. As time has gone on it has instead turned into something precious, like diamonds.' Understanding support makes all the difference as hard-pressed people slowly find relief.

Our everyday lives will be illuminated as we learn to look below the surface and find more examples of gain from pain. The humble toothpaste tube requires pressure to make it productive, until it is curled up and empty. Of course, we should try to take a break before reaching that point ourselves! Fatigue is another trigger for irritability, so watchful friends may need to get alongside and, when they can, lighten the load.

TRUSTING WHEN WE CANNOT SEE

So often we find it easier to complain than to look for any possible good arising from the little trials of every day. A spoilt meal, a mislaid document, traffic jams, a wet day, an intrusive telephone call, or running late for an appointment, these and other minor interruptions in our planned routines can leave us irritated and upset. Many of us are ready to turn to the Lord for help when coping with great disappointment, illness or different kinds of bereavement. Why should we leave him out when we get behind the wheel of a car, or when the clock seems to be going too fast, or when our hopes of a quiet evening or plans for a productive morning are dashed? For many, the daily grind seems to go by on an endless treadmill of duty or drudgery with no thought of him, unless to complain about him.

Despite knowing this in our heads, it is not natural to stay positive about such daily difficulties. Yet to try to keep remembering the amazing love and watchful care of God is to find his Spirit's help to change our focal distance. Instead of concentrating on the immediate discomfort, we learn to trust to his long-term creative purpose through it. Why do we ever grumble and show discontent at events our loving Lord has permitted? Yes, life inescapably brings hurts, small and greater. We may have learned to lean back on his strength in the bigger trials but it is in the petty ones that we tend to fall down. Writing to the quarrelsome, discontented young church at Corinth, Paul cited the many times that the Israelites grumbled in the wilderness, provoking God's wrath for what he clearly regarded as sinful. We are warned not to indulge! (1 Cor. 10: 10–11)

Basically, such resentment is frequently the response of an over-inflated 'capital I'. We need to cooperate with his Spirit and consciously train ourselves not to react so hastily, but instead to respond to the opportunities for more self-control. Easier said than done!—especially for those with a short fuse or who are simply exhausted. Turning to God, trusting for his gifts of patience and peace, is a way both to please and to glorify him. This may sound like an impossible ideal but all our lives long we will have plenty of opportunities to work at it. We work out what God works in (Phil. 2: 12–13).

POSITIVE SIDE EFFECTS OF PAINS AND PRESSURES

Problems and pains of different kinds are experienced throughout the whole of humanity, yet some are able to put their tragedies to gainful purpose. Parents of a dead teenager donated his organs to save others. His grieving mother later met the recipient of her son's heart, a young man very grateful for the costly permission that had bequeathed it to him. He placed the mother's hand on his chest where she was thrilled to feel the steady heartbeat, a vital part of her lost son still working well.

It is easy to overlook such creative responses among all the bad news from which no obvious good has yet emerged. As we learn to look behind the headlines, encouraging little pictures shine out like stars even when the big picture is still dark. An older sister holds a little brother's hand as they wander through a bomb site looking for home. A starving mother gives food to her hungry children, not knowing whether the aid parcel will hold enough for her as well. A local community rallies round to help shocked families when the tower block where they and their loved ones had lived went up in flames. Less newsworthy are terminally ill believers whose quietly unfaltering faith encourages others.

People already suffering can often teach us the most if we are ready and humble enough to learn from them. The story of Jesus' death and resurrection continues to set the divine pattern of something outwardly bad (his betrayal and crucifixion) bringing forth a much greater good (our salvation and his subsequent exaltation.) This creative pattern can often be traced in both the small and great crises of our own lives. It takes time and trust to perceive it, but makes all the difference when we do.

ALL FOR HIS SAKE

In 1633 George Herbert wrote a poem, later set to music as a hymn, which began:

> Teach me, my God and King
> In all things thee to see,
> and what I do in anything
> to do it as for thee.

From 'The Elixir' by George Herbert

He suggests that doing all 'for thy sake' completely transforms a mundane task such as sweeping a room. Offering the chore to God 'makes that and the action fine'. If we were to take to heart that ancient wisdom we would find that our Lord shares and sweetens the heavy load. He helps us to overcome our natural inclination for self-pity and complaint. The daily offering could include 24-hour care of a demented dear one; facing an unruly class of reluctant pupils; a routine and repetitive job; uncongenial workmates; a queue of people still to be seen past closing time; a daily trek to find water and then wearily carrying it home. Even constant debilitating and nagging pain comes into Herbert's 'all things'. We do well to recall and acknowledge that in everything our Lord reigns supreme (Col. 1: 18).

The daily grind and common task give frequent opportunities for us to quit grumbling and instead to offer up the unwelcome assignment as a form of sacrifice to the one who has allowed it. For most of us, the writer included, learning this kind of response takes a long time and lots of experience. We slowly begin to recognise the nudge of the Holy Spirit, reminding us that '...the Spirit helps us in our weakness' (Rom. 8: 26).

We recall how the British Queen acknowledges the gruelling training necessary before her troops can give her such a worthy offering. Her appreciation makes it all worthwhile. How much more wonderful it will be if, after offering up a lifetime of pains and pressures to our King, we are each welcomed into his kingdom to hear him say, 'Well done, good and faithful servant' (Matt. 25: 21).

FROM TEDIUM TO TE DEUM

A Latin hymn from the fourth century starts with *'Te Deum laudamus'*, meaning, 'Thee, O God, we praise'. It is still sung in many churches today, usually known simply as 'the Te Deum'. To make this the theme song of our lives would be to change tedium into *Te deum*—a worthy offering of worship to the King of kings.

READ, MARK, LEARN
Zechariah 13: 9
2 Corinthians 11: 23–28
1 Corinthians 10: 10, 12–13
Philippians 2: 5–11
2 Corinthians 1: 8–11

BACKGROUND READING

Carmichael, Amy, *Gold by moonlight* (London: SPCK, 1935)

Greene, Mark and Catherine Butcher, *The servant Queen and the King she serves* (Swindon: Bible Society, HOPE and LICC, 2016)

Herbert, George, 'The Elixir' in *The works of George Herbert*, ed. by F. E. Hutchinson (Oxford: Clarendon Press, 1941), p. 184

Packer, J. I., *Knowing God* (London: Hodder & Stoughton, 2005)

Roseveare, Helen, *Give me this mountain* (Tain, Ross-shire: Christian Focus Publications, 2006)

CHAPTER 17

Storing up treasure in heaven

THE APOSTLE John wrote of a series of great revelations he had received during his exile on the Isle of Patmos. He was there as punishment for expressing his faith in the Lord Jesus Christ, but he used the isolation to write his book, Revelation. Commentaries on it abound. They need to be read in conjunction with some of Jesus' statements (Matt. 24: 3–44 and John 6: 39–40), Isaiah 60, and Paul's reporting (remembering that he was probably the 'man in Christ' who had seen a vision of paradise) (2 Cor. 12: 1–4; 1 Thess. 4: 14–18 and 1 Cor. 15: 51–52). As tends to be the case with dreams, the timescale for fulfilment of John's visions is not clear but it seems that, at the completion of this age, time as we know it will be no more. In the continuing love and service of our Lord Jesus Christ we are assured that everlasting spiritual life will surmount physical death (John 3: 16).

OUR DESTINATION UNVEILED

John first shares his great revelation about the state and fate of seven different young churches. In chapters 4 and 5, he gives an account of his vision concerning the destination of those whose earthly lives have been devoted to the Lord Jesus and spent in his service. These faithful ones will enter his presence at their journey's end; indeed, the future hope of all believers is to be with him for evermore. Many years before, John had introduced two of his own disciples to the incarnate Jesus, giving him the title 'Lamb of God'. (John 1: 29) In heaven his followers' gaze will be fixed on the same Lamb, once slain but gloriously ascended to his throne. He will still bear scars that speak of past suffering ('a Lamb looking as if it had been slain'.) At his wounded feet we will kneel in humble worship, life's trials behind us (Rev. 5: 6–14).

John does his best to describe the glories of heaven as seen in his vision but leaves us bedazzled and overwhelmed. Glory radiates from the throne of God and of the Lamb, our Lord Jesus Christ. He who once was slain is enthroned as Lord of countless multitudes, the greatest possible gain arising out of the most profound pain. In his presence many voices will be raised to proclaim glory, honour and power to God and the Lamb.

At the start of John's account Satan had not yet met his end and would inflict further persecution on believers, as he still does today. This calls for patient endurance and faithfulness. For their testimony to Jesus and the word of God some would be beheaded (right up to our own times) but then be the first to rise and reign with Christ (Rev. 20: 4–5). Satan will be temporarily imprisoned, but on his release will make a final desperate attempt to deceive the nations and threaten God's people. The plot will fail, he will finally be overthrown and his evil powers finished in unquenchable flames (Rev. 20: 7–10).

THE DAY OF JUDGMENT

God's judgment will evidently follow the pattern outlined by Jesus in his story about the separate destinations of 'sheep' (his all-loving followers) from that of 'goats' (neglectful of others as they pursue their own way) (Matt. 25: 31–46). Only those committed to the Lamb will be found recorded in his book of life and spared to see the drama to come (Rev. 20: 11–15).

We have little preaching and teaching today about the prospect of future judgment, yet Jesus often referred to it. In his parable the unrepentant 'goats' face the prospect of eternal punishment instead of being granted eternal life. Jesus said that sinners who deliberately reject his offer of forgiveness will in turn be banished from God's presence. We would prefer to focus on God's unique and generous compassion. Yet in his justice and righteousness—and compassion—he has already provided a wonderful way of escape from the death penalty. To treat this with contempt arouses his 'wrath', an expression of his justice (Rom. 2: 5–8).

Judgment for the 'sheep' will be concerned with what they have built on the foundation of their faith in Jesus' atoning sacrifice. Have they just said, 'Thank you Lord,' but then been less than wholehearted in following him? Any shoddy work offered to him will be burnt up, like mere wood, hay or straw, although the workers themselves will be spared (1 Cor. 3: 10–15). As long as earthly life lasts, we must surely want to give him of our best in grateful response to his loving mercy and grace. We do not want to be ashamed when he welcomes us to the place made ready for us.

God's commands are not dictatorial but they are clear. His loving design is for them to give the best possible lives to those who choose to obey them. With the help of his Spirit we slowly learn not to kick against his words but to discover how wise, kind and life-giving they are.

NO MORE PAIN

The last two chapters of John's book of Revelation are concerned with the final establishment of a new heaven and earth, as prophesied by Isaiah centuries ago (Isa. 65: 17–25). It will come about when our Lord Jesus Christ returns and reigns. As members of the Church, described as the bride of Christ, his followers will take up residence with him in a renewed Jerusalem, the Holy City of God. We shall than see for ourselves exactly what John's description foretells (Rev. 21: 1–5). He writes in terms of a literal city with gates, streets and walls but we have to wait to discover the reality!

Human minds cannot imagine more than some kind of worshipping community on a densely populated Planet Heaven but, 'What no eye has seen, what no ear has heard, and what no human mind has conceived—the things God has prepared for those who love him' (1 Cor. 2: 9). The one who created our amazing universe will have perfect preparations in hand for his new heaven and earth.

We are given wonderful promises about life in the new home: 'Look! God's dwelling place is now among the people and he will dwell with them...He will wipe every tear from their eyes. There will be no more death or mourning or crying or pain, for the old order of things has passed away' (Rev. 21: 3–4). *'No more pain'!* What gain! Those who have lived depraved and dissolute lives will be excluded from these joys, having persistently ignored Jesus' sacrificial offer of forgiveness. Their end is described as a second death. (Rev. 21: 8) For the rest there will be vibrant everlasting life.

TRANSFORMATION OF EARTHLY TRIALS ADDS TO HEAVEN'S GLORY

John goes on to describe more about this indestructible city. There are so many echoes of the thoughts we have reflected on in previous chapters. We have considered examples of the many ways in which we may see gain coming from pain as we learnt to look beyond what is seen to what at first we had not seen. Jesus cited childbirth as an experience when a mother forgets her labour pains in the joyful delivery of her child, a positive result from a painful experience. We considered the possibility of a similar effect when faith is sustained through various kinds of trial, ranging from the sheer grind of every day routine to intense persecution and martyrdom. We have met some of those 'who in this transitory life are in trouble, sorrow, need, sickness, or any other adversity' (Church of England, 1975, p. 302). Some later found blessings coming from their experiences of suffering when at the time it had seemed that God had forgotten them. For many, if not most, the secret of their emergence from shadow to sunshine lay in the support they had received, both practical and spiritual. God's Spirit, often speaking through his word, provides a never-ending source of strength, and so do his people.

As we think back to some of the past examples we have considered together, it is fascinating (at least to me!) to find them re-appearing on a larger scale in the descriptions of the Holy City. They can be found in John's visionary book (Rev. 21 & 22). Whether literal or metaphorical, the details are rich with implications. We read how the enthroned Lamb (Light of the World) is its lamp (no more confusion, darkness or blindness), its twelve gates are huge pearls (developed through multiple pains), its foundation is of precious jewels (many of them produced under pressure) and the great streets are made of pure gold (refined in the furnace of affliction). Not only is this gold pure but it is transparent (suggestive of earlier severe hammering.) The quantities involved perhaps indicate that many sufferers have contributed to them, the contribution of each adding to the glory of the whole. Each one had offered the pain to God as a living, willing and loving sacrifice. He allowed their great trials and was to be entrusted with the rich outcome. What a thrill to find that the glory of the city was enhanced by so much past suffering offered up to him.

The gates of pearl are always open (no more exclusion or imprisonment), the tree-lined river flows with fresh water (no more thirst or famine), the leaves of those trees bring healing to the nations (no more sickness, disability, injustice, trafficking, terrorism, persecution, war or camps for refugees). Nothing has access to the city that would spoil it and there is not a wits' end corner to be turned. The servants of God-and-the-Lamb will delight to serve him (no more unemployment or daily grind) and they will reign with him for evermore (no more uncertainty, oppression or depression.) The trials of our earthly lives will be forgotten in the splendour of what the Creator has made out of them. All things have been made new, troubles transformed into treasures, to the glory of God.

TREASURE IN HEAVEN

John's main purpose in recording his vision is to portray the greatness of our glorious God and of the Lamb, splendidly enthroned together in heaven. Under this divine authority all forms of evil will be defeated. Added to that, the detailed plan of the city, specifying each part's precious components, gives further insight into a number of Bible passages. Malachi speaks of the day when the Lord Almighty will make up his 'treasured possession,' (the King James' Authorised Version specifies 'jewels') (Mal. 3: 17). Psalm 116 declares, 'Precious in the sight of the Lord is the death of his faithful servants' (Ps. 116: 15). Could the same thoughts have been in Jesus' mind when he spoke about storing up treasure in heaven, not on earth? (Matt. 6: 19–21)

If we have few earthly treasures, or give them away, Jesus said that we are not to worry about finding enough food and clothing. In his recorded words he reminds us that our heavenly Father knows all that we genuinely need. He will supply that and more when we make his priorities our own (Matt. 6: 25–34). Those who first heard these words probably thought of heavenly treasure in terms of temple offerings but, having come from heaven to earth, Jesus knew what 'glorious riches' he had left there and still longs to share with us (Phil. 4: 19).

It grieved Jesus that some found his teaching too hard to follow (Mark 10: 17–23). The cost was too high then and many find it to be so still. Yet, looked at another way, any suffering that believers may undergo will, if offered up to God, be changed. It may contribute to the gold and precious stones that adorn the heavenly city. On earth, generous donors are sometimes proud to see their names gratefully engraved on a public yet essentially impermanent building. How much greater a surprise and delight it will be to find how many of our unidentified but accumulated pains have been transformed to add to the glory of God's heavenly home. All honour will then be his, not ours.

SURPRISED BY JOY

There is a special depth here and now to the joys of our Christian fellowship worldwide. We will know even greater joy when the hope set before us is fulfilled and we go to be with the Lord. It is no mere mocker's 'pie in the sky when you die' that awaits us but the place with him that he has promised to prepare for us. Until then he intends us to live life to the full (John 10: 10). Total capacity will be reached when he finally invites us to go home with him. How wonderful it will be to have no earthly distractions ahead to spoil all the heavenly joys to come.

At the centre of the Holy City will be our Lord Jesus who has taken us safely there and welcomes us through wide open gates. In the penultimate chapter of his book, John describes a perfect marriage, arranged between him (the Lamb) and the residents of the city, the company of believers. In ways beyond our understanding, it seems that this signals a fully restored companionship between God and his totally committed, beloved and loving people. The imagery is of a completely compatible and indivisible relationship, never to be threatened again (Rev. 21: 2–3). Best of all will be to live for ever with the Lord, for that is his promise and on it we build our hope, even when the going gets tough down here.

Until we reach that ultimate destination, come what may come, we are promised strength for today and bright hope for tomorrow. What great gain it will be in the end to find that pain is no more. The time for its creative work will be over because God's purposes have then been fulfilled. No wonder the book of Revelation ends with the prayer, 'Come, Lord Jesus'. Until he gathers us to himself, either through death or on the day of his return, we remain blessed by his grace. With John, we can say a loud 'Amen' to that. So be it (Rev. 22: 20–21).

READ, MARK, LEARN

1 Corinthians 2: 9–10
Revelation 4: 1–2
Revelation 5: 13–14
Matthew 25: 31–46
Revelation 20: 11–12
Malachi 3: 16–17
Revelation 22: 12–14, 17, 20

BACKGROUND READING

Church of England, The, 'The Order of the Administration of the Lord's Supper' in *The Book of Common Prayer* (Oxford: Oxford University Press, 1975)

Mallard, Paul, *Invest your suffering: Unexpected intimacy with a loving God* (Nottingham: InterVarsity Press, 2013)

Packer, J. I., *Finishing our course with joy: Ageing with hope* (Nottingham: InterVarsity Press, 2014)

Wilcock, Michael, *The message of Revelation* (Leicester: InterVarsity Press, 1975)

Last word

EARLIER CHAPTERS have illustrated the possibility of gain quietly developing through the painful experiences of different people in different ways. The benefit has often been in the spiritual realm, so is rarely acknowledged as important by those with little spiritual perception. They see only the tragedy without the triumph that may accompany or follow great trials. Even the sufferers themselves do not always realise until long afterwards how God had been at work through their dark times. Tear-filled eyes find it hard to see how any good at all can arise out of the pain that caused them.

Those with experience of God's ways will trust where they cannot see, whilst those new to suffering have this lesson still to learn. For all of us, it usually takes the gift of hindsight to glimpse more of the hidden but creative purposes of God. From the beginning, the Creator had designed human beings to be made in his image (Gen. 1: 27). This likeness was eventually illustrated by God-made-flesh as the man Christ Jesus (Col. 1: 15). God stays quietly at work in our troubles with the great intention of conforming us to the image of his Son (Rom. 8: 29). Early in human history the image was marred by disobedience, but through Christ it can be regained. Our ultimate expectation is to see him in person and then to be made like him, the lost image completely restored (1 John 3: 2 and Phil. 3: 20–21). Nothing could be better than that!

Meanwhile, we trust to his grace and cling to his love. In time we may thank him for lessons learned in our valleys. In God's gracious hands, great gains may have slowly emerged from those past pains. Even better, our new insights can overflow to enrich other lives.

WE REST ON THEE

Edith Gilling Cherry died when only 25 years old. After suffering from poliomyelitis as an infant and a stroke at the age of twelve she spent most of her life on crutches. During her short, disabled life she was enabled to become a noted writer of hymns, most written before she was 15 years old. Yet when dying she mourned that what she had done for her Lord seemed so small. Assured that her songs would live after her, she said that they had come to her fully formed, 'All I had to do was write them down.' She had no idea what a blessing they would be to so many, then and since. Perhaps Edith's best-known hymn today is the one sung in 1956 by five American missionaries, called to minister to the previously unreached Auca Indians of Ecuador. All five were put to death by those they had hoped to bring to eternal life.

This is what they sang:

> We rest on Thee, our Shield and our Defender:
> We go not forth alone against the foe;
> Strong in Thy strength, safe in Thy keeping tender,
> We rest on Thee and in Thy Name we go.
>
> Yes, in Thy Name, O Captain of salvation!
> In Thy dear Name, all other names above;
> Jesus, our Righteousness, our sure Foundation,
> Our Prince of glory and our King of love.
>
> We go in faith, our own great weakness feeling,
> And needing more each day Thy grace to know;
> Yet from our hearts a song of triumph pealing;
> We rest on Thee and in Thy Name we go.
>
> We rest on Thee, our Shield and our Defender:
> Thine is the battle, Thine shall be the praise
> When passing through the gates of pearly splendour,
> Victors, we rest with Thee through endless days.

Edith Gilling Cherry (1872–1897)

GAIN FROM PAIN

Was Edith's short, disabled life not worth living? Her songs have brought inspiration and encouragement to countless people across the world.

Were the lives of five healthy and brave young men thrown away and wasted? The widow of Jim, one of the young Americans, remembered that he had once written in his journal: 'He is no fool who gives what he cannot keep to gain that which he cannot lose.' Elisabeth Elliot wrote the story in a best-selling book, its title reflecting the focus of the song sung by the men as they faced death (Elliot, 2015). To be a widowed mother in such circumstances would have had many heading for the safety of the homeland. Instead, she shared Jim's commitment and courageously stayed on at the same mission station, continuing the work left unfinished by the five martyred men.

Later she was able to report how the very tribesmen who had murdered the young missionaries later came to share their faith in Christ. Mission was eventually accomplished. The seed sown in death had finally borne fruit in transformed Aucan lives. The words of Jesus were completely fulfilled: 'Very truly I tell you, unless a kernel of wheat falls to the ground and dies, it remains only a single seed. But if it dies, it produces many seeds.' (John 12: 24)

Like Edith Cherry's songs, Elisabeth Elliot's encouraging books have gone around the world. They have inspired many others to offer themselves freely in God's service, whatever the cost. A great harvest still follows the sowing of seeds by those who died as they planted them. Gain continues to emerge from their pain, for God's purposes are always good.

To quote the great missionary doctor Helen Roseveare, 'God never uses a person greatly until he has wounded him deeply. The privilege he offers you is greater than the price you have to pay.' From her own painful experiences, she knew what she was talking about.

'Therefore we do not lose heart. Though outwardly we are wasting away, yet inwardly we are being renewed day by day. For our light and momentary troubles are achieving for us an eternal glory that far outweighs them all. So we fix our eyes not on what is seen, but on what is unseen, since what is seen is temporary, but what is unseen is eternal' (2 Cor. 4: 16–18).

READ, MARK, LEARN
Zephaniah 3: 17–20
Psalm 23: 6

BACKGROUND READING

Cherry, Edith Gilling, 'We rest on Thee, our shield and our defender!' (1895), in *Songs of Fellowship*, Vols 1–4 (Eastbourne, East Sussex: Kingsway, 2010), no. 584

Elliot, Elisabeth, *Through gates of splendour: The five missionary martyrs of Ecuador* (Milton Keynes: Authentic Media, 2015)

Roseveare, Helen, *Living sacrifice: Willing to be whittled as an arrow* (Tain, Ross-shire: Christian Focus Publications, 2007)

'Janet Goodall writes after a lifetime of caring for children, parents and siblings who face inexplicable suffering. From their experiences and those of others she sees the extraordinary power of the Christian gospel to bring blessing and newness of life, even from unlikely beginnings. Essential reading for all those who face any kind of suffering and for those who walk beside them.'
John Wyatt, Emeritus Professor of Neonatal Paediatrics, Ethics and Perinatology at University College London

'In *Gain from Pain,* Janet Goodall has bravely articulated what some of us believe but dare not say lest we are thought to be heartless and insensitive. She has very helpfully drawn on her professional experience and personal faith to say that in the face of pain and suffering God has never left or forsaken us. The message behind the ugly tapestry of Good Friday and the dark and silent Holy Saturday is that Easter Sunday and the resurrection are around the corner. That is where our hope lies. This book may be just what you need to find the help God gives.'
Margaret Sentamu, Leadership Development Consultant

'Janet Goodall is a storyteller with a purpose. She has seen many families find hidden treasure along with their painful experiences. She hopes that the reader will discover this same treasure.'
Jeremy Lefroy, former Member of Parliament, Stafford constituency

'Whether you are struggling with pain or trying to comfort others, this book is for you. From years of helping children and their families through illness, disability, dying and bereavement Janet Goodall has built up a wealth of experience and wisdom which she passes on to us.'
Janet Lefroy PhD FRCGP, General Practitioner and Senior Lecturer, Keele University School of Medicine

www.ingramcontent.com/pod-product-compliance
Lightning Source LLC
Chambersburg PA
CBHW071240070526
44583CB00017B/2262